Questions About ...

The Greatest Mysteries of Life

And

Beyond Life

Questions About ...

The Greatest Mysteries of Life

And

Beyond Life

God, Spirit, Soul, Religion, Love, Life,
Future, War, Death, Dying, Afterlife

By

Lynn Brown, PsyD

Questions About…

The Greatest Mysteries of Life

And

Beyond Life

Copyright © 2018 by Lynn Brown, PsyD.

All rights reserved.

No portion of this book may be reproduced, distributed, or transmitted in any form or by any means, including photocopying, recording, or other electronic or mechanical methods without permission from the author or publishing company.

For permissions or to contact the author email:

LCBWrites@outlook.com

Printed in the United States of America

ISBN-13: 978-1882589081

ISBN-10: 1882589084

Published by:

LCB Writes Book Publications, LLC.

LCBW

Austin, Texas

Dedication

The book is dedicated to all those who seek to find their answers to their "*Questions About... The Greatest Mysteries of Life and Beyond Life*".

Acknowledgement

I applaud the courage and acknowledge all those who have preceded me and those who are currently sharing their answers to these questions so I too could arrive at my answers to the "*Questions About…The Greatest Mysteries of Life and Beyond Life*".

Table of Contents

Introduction 1

God 4

    Is there a God?   4

    What if I don't believe in God?   4

    What Is God?   4

    Where did God Come from?   4

    What does God look like?   5

    Why can't we see God?   5

    Is God male or female?   5

    Why doesn't God just appear on Earth for all to see and hear?   6

    How can God be at one place at all times?   6

    What does God want?   7

    What does God do?   7

Space-Time Continuum 8

    What Is the Space-Time Continuum which God created?   8

    Why did God create everything in the Space-Time Continuum?   8

    If God can create the universe, why can't God encompass all feelings and emotions?   9

    How does the creation of the space-time continuum allow God to understand through experience?   10

Spirit/Soul 12

    What is a spirit?   12

    What is a soul?   12

    What Is subconscious, conscious, and superconscious?   12

    Are a soul and spirit the same thing?   13

How does the spirit/soul experience everything for God?	13
Why did God create human beings?	13
Is the soul/spirit's sole purpose to experience life for God?	14
What is the soul's mission?	14
What is the spirit's mission?	14
Why is achieving the highest level of consciousness and fulfillment so important?	15
How does the body, mind, and spirit/soul triad reach a higher level of consciousness?	16
Are the mind and body robots of the soul?	17
Can one's profession be the spirit's mission?	18
What state of being is the soul seeking through one's profession?	18
Can being in the state of love create worldly success?	18
Is a decision bad if it's not in alignment with the spirit's mission?	19
Does the soul influence the mind to make decisions aligning with the spirit's mission?	19
How does the soul create these situations?	20
What about feedback and the influences of people?	20
How does one get in touch with feelings and emotions?	21
What is our internal voice?	21
What does the spirit do when the mind consistently makes decisions not in alignment with the spirit's mission?	22
What happens if the spirit does not make it back when the body wakes up?	22
Does the spirit/soul ever give up on the mind/body decision process?	23
Is Earth a school for the spirit/soul to learn and feel?	23
Freedom of Choice..	24

Is it acceptable to do whatever we want while on Earth? 24
Is it OK to do bad things? 25

Right and Wrong 26

What determines if something is right or wrong? 26

How can the same thing be seen as both right and wrong depending upon the observer? 26

Is a belief system the same as religion? 26

How can we change someone's opinion about what is right or wrong? 27

How is everyone's interpretation of what's right and wrong formed? 27

What determines whether something is actually right or wrong? 27

Why are there so many bad people in the world? 28

Why do people make bad decisions? 28

How can stealing, killing, or harming a child be right? 29

Is it right to abort a fetus? 31

Doesn't the fetus's soul have a say about being aborted or not? 32

Why would the soul of the fetus want to be aborted? 32

Does a spirit decide who its parents are going to be? 32

Is it ever right to kill another human? 33

Why would someone's belief system allow someone to kill another? 33

If actions only fulfill one's belief system, why do people go to jail for their actions? 34

If there are no wrong decisions, can we do anything and everything we want? 34

How can we only make right decisions and end up living in poverty 34

What about children born into extreme poverty?   35

What if we break God's law?   36

Doesn't God send people to Hell if God's laws are broken?   36

Did Genghis Khan and Hitler go to Heaven?   36

Decision Making 38

How do we know when we're making the right decisions during our lifetime   38

Why do I sometimes have a hard time deciding or procrastinate?   38

What happens after the consequences are known?   40

How can a choice that was not favorable become the right choice?   42

Are all decisions and choices ultimately the right choice no matter the consequences?   43

What about when a quick decision is needed?   44

Which decisions represent love and which are represented by fear?   44

Selfishness 45

Shouldn't all decisions be unselfish decisions?   45

What is healthy selfishness?   45

What is unhealthy selfishness?   46

What causes us to make unhealthy selfish decisions and choices?   47

How are unhealthy selfish decisions and choices tied into fear?   47

How can fear act as a demotivator?   47

What can I do to make love-based decisions?   48

Forgiveness 50

What is the definition of forgiveness?   50

When is it possible to forgive the perpetrator of the malicious and harmful act?   50

Isn't it wrong not to forgive someone?	50
How can we move on with our lives without forgiving perpetrators of pain?	51
Why is it important to reach a state of release?	51
How does one achieve a state of release?	51
How can there be a possible reason or purpose for someone acting out a malicious and harmful act?	53
How is it possible to forgive the perpetrator of the malicious and harmful act?	54
How does the perpetrator of a harmful act arrive at a place of being forgiven?	54
Why does God allow malicious and harmful acts to occur?	54

Death and Dying 55

What is death and what happens when we die?	55
Does our spirit ever die?	55
Who decides the time of our death?	55
Isn't it wrong to commit suicide and won't we go to Hell?	55
What about medical-assisted death and euthanasia?	56
When does the superconscious (soul/spirit) decide when to die?	56
Who decides the time of death in accidents and natural disasters?	56
Why is it important to understand death?	57
Could I live a life of peace if I don't understand death?	57
What happens if someone never understands death?	57
Why is there so much sadness and grief over the passing of a loved one?	57
What happens when we die?	58
If one has fulfilled its purpose in life, can the spirit go back and visit loved ones?	61

What happens during Phase 2 for believers?	61
Is God just a light or does God have a physical form?	65
Why is it important to see both movie viewings?	66
What happens if, after viewing both movies, my life's purpose(s) was not fulfilled?	66
Can I kill myself to avoid something and then return to avoid it?	68
My soulmate died; why haven't they come back to me?	68
Can everyone who dies in a mass death be experiencing their purpose in life?	69
Why choose going back to Earth to avoid death rather than go to Heaven?	69
Why don't I remember experiencing Phase 3 after returning to my life?	70
What will happen next after viewing the first two movies of my life?	70
What happens when I reach Heaven?	74
Where is our Heaven?	76
Why did God create Heaven?	77
Do animals go to Heaven?	77
Are there angels in Heaven?	77
What do angels do?	77
How long can I stay in Heaven?	77
Why would anyone want to leave Heaven?	78
What happens during Phase 5: communion?	78
How does the spirit know what it wants to experience or do prior to reincarnation?	80
What can be learned by understanding the five phases of death?	81
What is God's grace?	82

Why do some people appear to have more of God's grace than another? 82

Why would anyone want to be born with a lifelong handicap or disease? 82

If we choose, why would anyone want to be homeless, living under a bridge? 83

Religions 85

Are religions bad? 85

Why do religions exist? 85

Why are there different religions? 86

What is the right religion? 86

Is it acceptable to be an atheist or agnostic? 87

War 88

Is there ever a good reason for a country to start a war? 88

What are the reasons for a country to get involved in a war? 88

Why do countries start wars against other countries? 88

What are ways to prevent wars from starting? 88

How can these situations and conditions be stopped to prevent wars? 89

What global organizations need to be modified? 89

What is the long-term solution to prevent social upheaval? 90

Cultural Conditioning 92

What is "belief system cultural conditioning?" 92

What is social cultural conditioning? 92

Integrity 94

What is individual integrity? 94

What is the definition of a person of high integrity? 94

How do we know when the choice is from the heart or mind?	94
Why is it important to live a life of high integrity?	95

Modifications To Cultural Conditioning 96

Why are modifications to social cultural conditions necessary?	96
What guideline should be used to determine what modifications are made?	96
What cultural modifications need to be made to promote world peace and harmony?	97
Why is it important for one to have a belief system?	103

Building Integrity 104

How can we instill integrity to reduce war, conflicts, and social upheaval?	104
How can I be a messenger of social and belief system cultural conditioning changes?	108
How can I have the greatest impact as a messenger?	108
How do I start a movement?	109

Emotions and Emotional Intelligence 111

What is emotional intelligence?	111
What are emotions and feelings?	111
Why is it important to know and build one's emotional intelligence?	111

We Are All One 113

How will understanding we are all one improve world condition?	113
What is meant by "we are all one," and how can we all be one?	113
What is preventing humanity from feeling we are all one?	114
How is social cultural conditioning preventing movement toward oneness?	115

How is belief system cultural conditioning preventing movement toward oneness?   115

How is one's level of integrity preventing movement toward oneness?   115

How is the spirit's mission on Earth preventing movement toward oneness?   115

So, the separation of humanity will always exist so we can understand oneness?   116

With so many different cultures, how can we become one?   116

Prayer 117

What is prayer?   117

How does a co-creation prayer work?   117

What is a prayer of thanksgiving?   117

What happens when a prayer is not answered?   118

If God answers all prayers, what happens when I pray for someone not to die and they do?   118

Why aren't prayers answered during our current lifetime?   118

How can prayers be so all powerful?   119

What is the best way to pray?   120

What should we pray about?   120

Love 121

What is love?   121

What are the positive physical actions of love?   121

What are the positive physical inactions of love?   122

What are the positive spoken words of love?   122

What are the positive unspoken words of love?   122

What does oneness mean as associated with the definition of love?   123

Are we love?	124
Is love a choice?	125
What is the purpose of love?	126
What is love to an atheist, agnostic, or some other form of non-theist belief?	126
What must be in place for love to occur?	127
How can one experience love?	127
Does love grow?	127
What is developmental love?	128
What is self-love?	130
What is human love?	130
What is Godly love?	131
What is unconditional love?	131
How can parents of murderers love their children unconditionally?	132
How does one begin loving themselves unconditionally from a spiritual state of being?	133

The Future 134

Will humans eventually eliminate themselves from the face of the Earth?	134
Why won't humans not eliminate themselves from the planet?	134
Do humans have the capability of destroying the Earth?	135
What is going to happen in the next 100 years?	135
What are artificial intelligence (AI) and super artificial intelligence machines?	136
How will AI and super-intelligent machines make a positive impact within the next 100 years?	136
How will humans become smarter and smarter?	137

If humans become smarter, won't we be on the same level as AI machines?	137
What about humans' negative environmental impact?	138
How can IT and AI be our way out of the existing and future problems?	138
Is it possible that artificial intelligence will create problems for humankind?	139
What will prevent intelligent machines from taking over the planet?	140
Won't AI superintelligence result in job loss?	140
Why won't there be any wars in the distant future?	141
Where does God and the human soul/spirit fit in the future?	143
Will there become a time when technology prevents humans from dying?	144
Will there ever be peace on Earth?	144
Conclusion..	*147*

Introduction

This book poses the great unanswerable questions that often plaque humanity. Some are questions I've asked myself and others I've heard debated among others. I've also collected the responses from a random assortment of people to the query: "*If we were in the presence of the ultimate authority who knew all the answers, what would we ask?*"

I arrived at my answers by talking to family, friends, acquaintances, and strangers—anyone with knowledge on each topic. As a youth, my parents exposed me to the Christian faith and, like most families of my generation, listened to all of the nationally broadcasted sermons by one of the first televangelist, Billy Graham. As a young adult, I listened to the late televangelist Robert H. Schuller preach during the Hour of Power television show and when I lived in southern California, I attended many of his services from my car at his drive-in church. The current service I watch is the weekly internet broadcasts by the ministers at Mile Hi Church in Denver, Colorado.

As a young adult, I was curious and compelled to explore the numerous other religious persuasions, and spiritualities, as well as atheism and agnosticism. I explored the major religions, including the major contexts/scriptures of the Quran of the Islamic faith, Bible of the Christian faith, the Four Vedas of the Hindu faith, as well as numerous texts of the Buddhist teachings. I also studied deeply into New Age Spirituality and attended services at some Unity Churches. I am currently a member of the Mile Hi Church in Denver, Colorado.

The authors of many of the spiritual-oriented books I have read and the ministers I have listened to and read about include Earnest Holmes, Robert H. Schuller, Eckhart Tolle, Deepak Chopra, Dr. Roger Teel, Dr. Patty Luckenbach, Rev. Barry Ebert,

The Greatest Mysteries of Life and Beyond Life

Rev. Cynthia James, Neal Donald Walsch, Marianne Williamson, and Sadhguru Jaggi Vasudev.

My answers to the questions presented in this book were crafted over the past sixty-plus years to arrive at what I feel in my heart are the right answers—stressing the *what I feel*. It's up to us, individually, to arrive at *what we feel* are the right answers based on our personal belief system. Our responses will often differ, which is perfectly correct. There is no one absolute right or wrong answer to any of these questions.

If there is no right or wrong answer but only our answers, what is the purpose of answering all of these questions? I believe it's vital for everyone to find a belief system. Whether it's through an organized religion, a personal morality code, or faith in a natural order of the universe, everyone needs something to fall back on when facing difficult times. Our answers will solidify and clarify our belief system and provide great comfort in life's journey.

One question that has been presented to me is what credentials or platform I have to be qualified to write such a book. Well, I have a bachelor's degree in mechanical engineering, a master's in business administration, and a doctorate in Psychology. I also have two more powerful degrees, an undergraduate degree in the "School of Hard Knocks" and a graduate degree in the "School of Hard Thoughts," while loving and living on this playground we call Earth. In my opinion, those of us who have experienced life to its fullest and have been around the block a few times can say there is no better education than living and experiencing life. That is why I take advantage of every opportunity to talk to an elderly person.

During my life span many of the beliefs expressed in this book have been challenged but my belief system has held steadfast. One major question I directly faced head on was, "*Is there life after death?*" I have faced and survived three bouts of cancer. During my second bout, there was an initial diagnosis of having Von Hippel-Lindau disease, which has a high mortality rate. Fortunately, it was ultimately a missed diagnosis, and correctly diagnosed kidney cancer, but there was a time period I lived with the thought of my life being cut short. Obviously, the thought of what will happen when I died crossed my mind heavily. Fortunately, the beliefs I have formed and expressed in this book held firm and I was at peace with death, if it was to occur.

Other life episodes that challenged my belief system included the death of my mom at an early age and not knowing my son, multiple major surgeries, having a brother experiencing the horrible effects of Alzheimer at an earlier than expected age, and a second brother that succumbed to AIDS at a relatively early age. These and many other life challenges triggered the same question of "WHY?" Fortunately, these experiences allowed me to come up with my answers and move forward in a healthy way, while fortifying my belief system.

My belief system was set, and as a result, I experienced immense relief and a profound sense of unfathomable inner peace - and I still do. That inner peace brought a level of calmness that reduced prolonged inner conflict. I perceived and felt life here on Earth differently, which made it more bearable. My daily challenges did not go away, nor did those challenges lessen the effect of sadness, anger, fear, joy, and other emotions. However, I was better equipped to face it and work through it all. Therefore, the purpose of this book and my hope and desire is to help others arrive at their own answers so they too can experience the serene inner peace of life.

GOD

Is there a God?

Yes, there is a God. There is, always has been, and always will be a God who is the great provider and creator of space-time, heavens, universes, and everything contained within, seen and unseen now, in the past, now, and in the future.

What if I don't believe in God?

If we don't believe there is a God while on Earth, that is acceptable to God. God will still be a part of a non-believer's life just as much as a believer's life. This may be hard for some people to believe, but God is one of total and complete unconditional love, unlimited compassion, and total forgiveness toward everyone no matter what we believe, what path we created during our lifetime, or what our thoughts, words, and actions were while on Earth.

What Is God?

God is the great eternal spirit with the highest level of consciousness, where there is unlimited and unconditional love, peace, and joy.

Where did God Come from?

God has always existed. This is a very hard concept for human beings to understand because we are programmed to believe that everything has a beginning, middle, and end. God is eternal.

What does God look like?

God is a spirit, and in Its purest form is an awe-inspiring, indescribable brilliant form of light.

Why can't we see God?

God in Its purest form is an awe-inspiring, indescribable brilliant form of light and our eyes does not have the capacity to see the "light image" of God. What we see while on Earth is not light itself but the reflection of light off an object. That physical limitation prevents us from seeing God in His pure form. In the spiritual realm where God lives, light is visible and thus God can be seen, not only as a brilliant light but in any shape or form God wishes to be in at a particular time.

Though the "light image" of God cannot be seen on Earth, what we can see is what God is. God is everything that is. There is nothing that God is not because God is everything we see. Just like Michelangelo is seen in the statute of David and on the Sistine Chapel ceiling, or Leonardo da Vinci is seen in all his inventions, God is the trees, the grass, the clouds, the rivers, the sun, the sky, the heavens, and everything else that can be seen because God created all there is.

Is God male or female?

God is female and male depending on the purpose at that moment and time. Gender is unimportant. What is important is that God just is.

Why doesn't God just appear on Earth for all to see and hear?

In what way could God appear that would convince all of humankind without a doubt that God is speaking? God could send someone to Earth who proclaims they were sent by God, but history has shown that people who proclaim to be God or sent by God are doubted, laughed at, and, in extreme cases, killed. God could yell out the answers for all to hear at once, in all the languages of the world, yet there would still be some people saying it wasn't God speaking but the devil. God could send a written document in all the different languages of the world, yet some people would still doubt it was God's writing. If God did talk or write to us, we would not believe it is God. People would refute it and proclaim it was some evil force, human or otherwise, trying to trick us to gain power and control over the world.

The point is that there is no way God could speak to all of humankind and convince humanity it was irrefutably, without a doubt, God speaking, telling us why we are here and giving answers to all the great questions of life. Even if we did believe God would physically appear and talk to us, the second reason God doesn't is that it would go against why God created everything.

How can God be at one place at all times?

Anything that is formless cannot be contained or restricted and can be in more than one place at one time. Given that God is formless, Its spirit cannot be contained or restricted and thus can be everywhere at one time. A good analogy is light from the sun. There is not a place on the surface of Earth that there is an absence of light over the course of a 24-hour day. Even in the middle of a cloud covered night, total darkness does not exist. So, if the light of the sun can be everywhere at one time, so too, then, can God, since God, in Its pure, natural state, is a light.

What does God want?

God does not have a need for anything and therefore does not have a want.

What does God do?

God is the great creator and provider of all that is seen and unseen and, after creation, became a co-creator. Prior to creating all there is, God initially existed alone with eternity and was nothing more than a tiny dot of unconceivable density. God then created from Its tiny existence everything seen and unseen with one big bang. The everything that God created during the Big Bang has been proven to exist by quantum physicists and has been labeled by Albert Einstein as the *space-time continuum*. Along with the continuum, God also created its daughter and son, or spirit pieces, who became co-creators with God.

Space-Time Continuum

What Is the Space-Time Continuum which God created?

The "space" within the space-time continuum is everything seen and unseen and, within this space, is everything that has happened, is currently happening, and will be happening in the future. We humans are currently creating and experiencing the moment of now in this space.

The "time" of the space-time continuum is not the seconds, minutes, and hours we use to measure the passage of time; it is our movement through the space.

The "continuum" in the space-time creation is the continuous and successive experiences and events that include the past, present, and future of everything seen and unseen. All the possible past, present, and future moments are occupying the continuum of space. From birth to death, spirits/souls are moving through this space along the path we create by the decisions we make. Even after we die, we are still part of the continuum but move from one dimension of the continuum to another. For those of us who don't believe in or have difficulty understanding the space-time continuum, there is a YouTube video produced by Nova that explains the concept in relatively simple terms. To find the video, Google *Time is an Illusion according to Einstein.*

Why did God create everything in the Space-Time Continuum?

Before everything seen and unseen was created, there was only God and nothing else. God conceptually knew of Itself as possessing unconditional love, infinite knowledge, and understanding of all there is, but lacked total awareness of unconditional love, infinite knowledge, and understanding. It is one thing to conceptually know something but, to truly understand something, it must be experienced and felt. The result of experiencing the feeling of the something is complete and total awareness. As an example, one can conceptually understand what it is like to lose a loved one, but until it is actually experienced and felt, one cannot achieve total awareness of the experience. Therefore, God could not experience and feel His unconditional love, infinite knowledge, and understanding because there was only God and nothing else.

In addition, polar opposites did not exist prior to creation, so without cold, God would not be able to understand what hot was. In order for tall to exist, its opposite, short, had to exist. In order for love to exist, hate had to exist.

In one Big Bang, God created everything in the space-time continuum in order to begin truly understanding all of Its unconditional love, infinite knowledge, and understanding through experience and polar opposites. Therefore, God created everything in the space-time continuum so that it can experience, feel, and become totally aware of all It knows conceptually.

If God can create the universe, why can't God encompass all feelings and emotions?

God understood what feelings and emotions were from a conceptual point of view before creating the universe but could not truly understand feelings and emotions until they were experienced. As an example, growing up, we conceptually understood love and the associated emotions and feelings by what we were told and read. It wasn't until we fell in love and experienced love that we could truly understand love and all its arrays of emotions. This is the reason why God created the universe and the space-time continuum. God wants to truly understand unconditional love, infinite knowledge, and understanding through experiences of the space-time continuum.

How does the creation of the space-time continuum allow God to understand through experience?

God created pieces of Itself called spirits. It was through the experiences of spirits in the space-time continuum on Earth that allowed God to experience and truly understand all It created. God does not directly feel the spirit's experiences when they occur in the space-time continuum. This only happens after our body and mind dies and our spirit returns to commune with God.

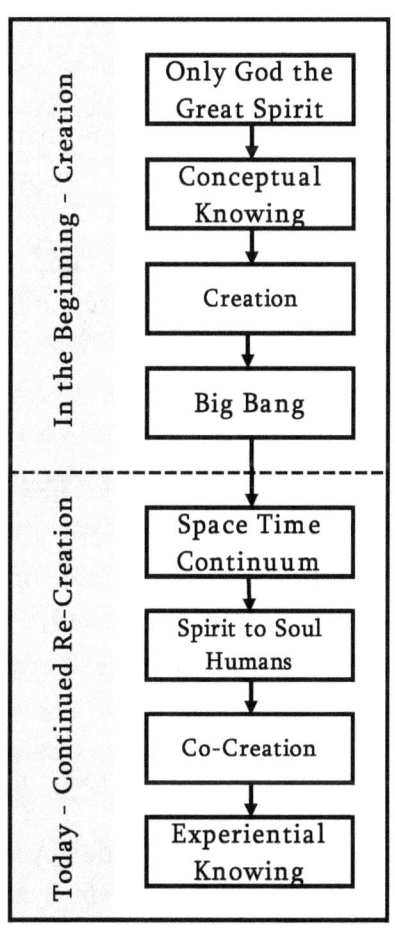

Spirit/Soul

What is a spirit?

God is the Great spirit who created daughter and son spirits. In their natural state, these spirits are a form of light that can take on physical features in the afterworld, when necessary. When the daughter and son spirits are incarnated with a human fetus at conception, that spirit becomes a soul. The soul reverts back to a spirit when it leaves the body upon death or when the mind is unconscious. Therefore, body, mind, and soul are finite but a spirit is infinite. Our spirit is essentially who we are and lives on forever and ever.

What is a soul?

A soul is a spirit that is incarnated into the fetus at conception, which is when a human being becomes a triad of body, mind, and spirit/soul comprised of one's conscious, subconscious, and superconscious. The body is the subconscious, our conscious resides in the mind, and our superconscious is our spirit/soul.

What Is subconscious, conscious, and superconscious?

The subconscious, conscious, and superconscious are the three levels that enable us to create, feel, and experience life based on the consequences of our decisions and choices. The subconscious level is where body functions are automatic, such as how the nervous system regulates life-sustaining functions, including breathing, heartbeat, etc. and less critical functions, such as blinking, sweating, and coughing. The instantaneous functions include fight-or-flight and jerking our hand back when touching a hot pan. The conscious level is the everyday awareness of our own mental processes, such as our feelings, sensations, and reality. The superconscious level is where our soul/spirit lives and is fully aware of the reason(s) for us to experience and feel while on Earth. The superconscious is constantly attempting to lead us to the right people, places, and activities in order to accomplish its mission on Earth.

Are a soul and spirit the same thing?

Yes, a soul is what a spirit is called when it becomes part of a human being. When the spirit becomes a soul, God is able to experience all It knows.

How does the spirit/soul experience everything for God?

When the spirit/soul becomes part of a human being, makes decisions, and acts on them, there are results and consequences. God eventually experiences what the spirit/soul experienced as well as what others experienced from the results and consequences. God does not experience these consequences while we are on Earth but after death.

Why did God create human beings?

Human beings were created as the vehicle for the soul/spirit and God to experience all there is. All human beings, regardless of our belief system, consists of a mind, body, and soul. God gave humans a mind, freedom of choice, and a body to carry out those choices. The soul experiences the consequences of our actions while on Earth, and God will experience the outcomes when the soul reverts back to a spirit in the afterlife.

Is the soul/spirit's sole purpose to experience life for God?

No. A spirit has the same reason for experiencing life's emotions and feelings as God. Spirits want to understand experimentally all they know conceptually. Since spirits are pieces of God, spirits too have all the knowledge of everything, but in order to truly understand all there is, it must be experienced. As the soul/spirit experiences life on Earth in the space-time continuum for God, it is also experiencing life for the spirit also. Therefore, the soul/spirit experiences life for God and itself in order to understand and experience all it knows.

The big difference between what God experiences and the spirit experiences is that God experiences life at a much greater rate. God experiences each spirit's experience, whereas the spirit only experiences its mission from one lifetime to the next.

What is the soul's mission?

The soul's mission is to experience what the spirit wishes to experience while on Earth. The experience can be a single event, a single feeling, multiple experiences, multiple feelings, etc. The soul's mission may not be just to experience something but also to be a messenger, provide a service, or teach a lesson to help other spirits fulfill their mission. So, it's important that the decisions the soul makes are in alignment with the spirit's mission while incarnated as a soul on Earth.

What is the spirit's mission?

The spirit's mission as a soul can have two purposes in a lifetime. The primary purpose is to experience something while incarnated as the soul of the human, which could include an event, a profession, a lifestyle, appearance, birthplace, specific parents, and so on. The list is endless.

God's desire for all spirits is to arrive at the highest level of consciousness and thus total fulfillment. The reason for the soul to experience something is that it allows the spirit to grow incrementally toward a higher level of consciousness and total oneness with God. The purpose of the human mind and body is to create a life in alignment with what the spirit desires to experience while incarnated as a soul in the body. Each soul's mission and experience are unique.

The spirit's second purpose in life is to be a messenger and/or teacher. Usually, these are spirits who have reached a higher level of consciousness and are on Earth to help other soul/spirits during their journey to a higher level of consciousness. Messengers and teachers also bring attention to other issues that need to be addressed or overcome to help humanity move constructively forward from a local and global perspective.

Why is achieving the highest level of consciousness and fulfillment so important?

At the highest level of consciousness and fulfillment, the spirit totally understands everlasting love, peace, joy, acceptance, gratefulness, and blessedness. Total fulfillment is God's wish for all of Its offspring. At this level, there is no place we need to be, nothing left to be accomplished, and nobody we have to be, except our true self.

To truly understand an experience, feeling, or emotion, we have to create the experience by making decisions of our own free will. Once the consequences of the decision have been felt, our soul can truly understand the experience. If someone just told us what to do, we will not truly understand or feel the experience. It's like the interaction between parents and their teenage children. There are times a parent tells a teenager what to do, or not to do. The teenager may understand conceptually what the parents are saying, but only when the teenager acts against the parent advice will they truly feel and understand the experience. How often have we experienced events that made us realize that our parents' insights were actually true?

We can also achieve purpose though close association with the experience. For example, if a very close friend or family member goes through an experience, we also indirectly feel the consequences. If our closest friend or one of their loved ones is attacked and seriously injured, we'll feel the same emotions and feelings they do. We can read all day about how to drive a car, but to fully understand the experience, we have to get behind the wheel. Similarly, we can hear others wax poetic about love but cannot relate until we love someone.

How does the body, mind, and spirit/soul triad reach a higher level of consciousness?

The mind and body start the process toward the spirit and God conceptually understanding all there is. The mind's role is to make a decision, and the body's role is to act out the decision. The spirit experiences the resulting action, emotion, and feeling of the decision. The body dies. The spirit is released from the body and enters into the afterlife, where God shares the spirit's experiences.

Even though billions of spirit/souls on Earth over millennia have repeatedly made the same types of decisions, God and the spirit don't get tired. No two people are identical. We are all unique. An identical decision made by many people creates different consequences, emotions, and feelings based on our unique set of circumstances, including culture, ethnicity, physical appearance, and level of enlightenment.

Are the mind and body robots of the soul?

No. The soul has no control over the human mind-body decision-making process. The soul does have the ability to create situations or guide the mind into making decisions in alignment with its mission. All humans consist of a body, mind, and soul. The soul will attempt to lead the mind-body and provide subtle input, but the human mind has the free will to make a decision and for the body to carry out the decision. Once the consequences of the decision have been felt, the human being can truly understand the experience. If the spirit/soul always told the mind-body what to do, the spirit/soul would not truly understand or feel the experience.

On the other hand, the body-mind cannot control the soul because the soul is without need. The soul always allows the body-mind the freedom of choice. The soul is a creating machine, and in order create and experience what It knows conceptually, the decision of the mind/body must be an act of its own will. Obedience is not creation but an involuntary response. Pure creation is initiated through free will.

Can one's profession be the spirit's mission?

Yes, but what we are being while we are doing our job is most important. Our soul cares about what we do for a living if it's part of the spirit's mission. If it is not, our soul really does not care and neither will we when our body-mind dies. If our profession is not part of our spirit's mission, the soul only cares about what we're being while we are doing. The mind/body is interested in satisfying its wants and needs, and the soul is interested in what we are being in order to succeed at what we are doing for a living.

What state of being is the soul seeking through one's profession?

One chooses their state of being no matter what their profession is. There are two states of being: love and fear. Love includes being open, honest, truthful, fair, caring, compassionate, sharing, understanding, and merciful. Fear includes being dishonest, greedy, inconsiderate, resentful, uncaring, bending the truth, distant, aloft, etc.

Two people can have equal skills, abilities, and education with the same job or profession, but those who choose a state of being of love will become successful and those who choose the state of being of fear won't. Choosing the right state of being applies to every profession; it's not the profession that makes one happy but the state of being while working.

Can being in the state of love create worldly success?

Being in a state of love will drastically increase our odds of worldly success, but keep in mind that worldly success is only a need of the mind-body. The feelings, rewards, and gifts derived of love will deliver a state of peace, fullness, emotional and spiritual richness. This state is so magnificent and rewarding that worldly goods and success will no longer be important.

The soul desires to make a life, not a living. It's an ironic truism of life that when worldly success and goods become of no concern to us, that's when worldly goods and success will flow to us.

Is a decision bad if it's not in alignment with the spirit's mission?

First of all, there is no such thing as a bad decision at the moment and time the decision is made. The mind always has a reason for why the decision was made; however, the consequences of the decision may result in perceiving the decision as bad or not in alignment with the spirit's mission. In this case, the decision can be looked at as a good decision because the mind has learned something from it. All experiences are good experiences for the soul/spirit.

Does the soul influence the mind to make decisions aligning with the spirit's mission?

Even though the mind makes the final decision, the soul does have indirect, nonverbal influence during the decision-making process. The soul speaks to the mind through intuition, emotions, and feelings. Intuitive decisions just feel right and we don't have any rational idea why. A gut decision is made through emotions and feelings created by the soul. Both are soulful forms of influence on the mind.

Other emotions used by the soul are happiness and joy. How does it feel when thinking about the options available with a decision? If the feeling is one of total happiness, one that speaks of truth, or one of love, then it is the soul speaking to us through feelings from the heart.

The soul also communicates thoughts through the heart to the mind. The soul will plant thoughts that produce a vision. The soul produces answers to the what-if in the light of total happiness, truth, and love.

How does the soul create these situations?

Have we ever made a decision that just felt right, but we didn't know why? That's an example of the soul's persuasion. The soul speaks to the human mind through feelings and intuition.

Another way the soul speaks is through events, minor or major, miraculous or devastating. Minor events could be making a wrong turn and seeing a billboard that makes us think, or hearing a song on the radio, which gives us a feeling that guides us in making a decision in alignment with the soul. A major event, such as the birth of a child, moving to another city, surviving a serious accident or illness, are samples of situations in which the soul speaks to the mind. Devastating occurrences can be a hurricane, tornado, or other natural disasters.

What about feedback and the influences of people?

It is strongly encouraged to gather information from family members, close friends, spiritual leaders, religious leaders, and other respected mentors. The feedback from any of them may be what is required to put us in touch with our feelings and emotions that will direct us to a soulful decision.

How does one get in touch with feelings and emotions?

To get in touch with our emotions and feelings, peacefully shift from our minds and our egos. It is important shift away from our ego because when decisions are based on the ego, the mind shuts off all emotions and feelings.

A place of peace is different for each one of us, but it must be where we can create some quiet time to quiet our minds and listen to our hearts. Most people initially seek out a quiet place with no distractions, such as a park, near a lake or ocean, or in their backyard. Our heart speaks the truth during those quite mind times.

Over time, it doesn't really need to be a quiet place. It can be anywhere because a place of peace is not really a place but a peace of mind. Masters of finding peace of mind can find it anywhere: in the middle of Time Square, at a sporting event, or in a subway station. In this place of peace, we are allowed to hear our internal voices.

What is our internal voice?

Some people call it our conscious; I believe it is our superconscious. We hear the internal voice when we are in a place of peace of mind. During a conversation with our superconscious, we will eventually feel the answer to whatever we're seeking. We'll know it once we hear it, and for most people, it's in the heart region or in the middle of their torso. I have heard terms such as abdominal brain and heart chakra to describe the location.

What does the spirit do when the mind consistently makes decisions not in alignment with the spirit's mission?

The spirit will become frustrated and overloaded. When that happens, the spirit escapes from being incarnated in the body during sleep, which is not only necessary for the body to function properly but is also a time when the soul can leave the body and be free. The soul does not need to be present when the body is sleeping. It can escape and recover from being bound to the body. When forced to do seemingly mundane and boring things, don't we feel sleepy? That is the soul/spirit speaking to us.

On the other hand, if we are making decisions in alignment with the spirit's mission, the spirit does not want to leave, which is why we can do something for hours on end without feeling tired. The soul speaks to us by making us sleepy when our soul is not happy with what we are doing. The soul makes us energized when we do something in alignment with the soul/spirit mission.

What happens if the spirit does not make it back when the body wakes up?

The spirit will always make it back no matter where it goes while the body is sleeping. The spirit is always in touch with the mind and body and will know when the body is waking. As the body starts to awaken, the spirit almost instantaneously travels back to the body. Even though Einstein's theory states nothing can travel at the speed of light, that only applies to objects with mass. Spirits are formless and without mass, so they can travel as fast or faster than the speed of light.

There are instances when there may be a slight amount of time when our spirit is both with us and away from us. It is for a brief moment, but I call this time the twilight zone; however, it is more commonly known as our dream state. It is during this time our spirit is dragging into our conscious the residue from where it came while we were asleep.

Does the spirit/soul ever give up on the mind/body decision process?

Yes, even though a spirit is very patient, there can become a time when the soul/spirit decides the ego/mind won't ever provide what it wants to experience. When this occurs, the spirit will create an event that causes the death of the body to release the spirit from the body and mind. This form of death is called spiritual suicide.

Is Earth a school for the spirit/soul to learn and feel?

Not really. Earth is more of a playground. The soul's mission is not to learn something. It's on Earth to experience something, to feel and understand. Therefore, a playground is a better description of Earth because it's where we feel free to create and do whatever we want.

FREEDOM OF CHOICE

Is it acceptable to do whatever we want while on Earth?

Yes, one of God's greatest gifts is freedom of choice. We all have this gift no matter our creed, race, color, social status, or the culture we live in. All too often, people feel they don't have a choice—especially when facing some severe challenge such as extreme poverty, a physical or mental disability, or abuse. They do have the freedom of choice on how to react to all situations.

A great example of this freedom of choice, no matter the situation is Victor Frankl, a holocaust survivor. During his captivity in World War II, the Germans took everything from him: his family, career, and dignity. They tortured him mercilessly, conducted hideous experiments on his body, confined him in a small cage where he could not stand or stretch out, kept him naked, and in pain. One day, he had a revelation: no matter what they did to him, they could not take away his freedom of choosing what to do and how to react to his situation.

Another great example of using the freedom of choice under dire circumstances is Harriet Tubman. Born in the 1820s into slavery, she could not read or write. She saw her siblings sold like livestock to other plantation owners. They were treated like a commodity and beaten on a regularly basis for minor issues. She was once struck in the head with a heavy metal object while trying to help another slave. The impact crushed her skull and left her unconscious for over a day. The severe concussion left her with lifelong bouts of vomiting, insomnia, and sleeping fits with visions.

Tubman could have easily given up, but like Victor Frankl, she knew no matter what the circumstances, we always have the freedom of how we choose to react. She eventually became one of the conductors of the Underground Railroad that helped many slaves escape to freedom. She was an abolitionist, a women's rights activist, and during the Civil War, was a scout, spy, and nurse.

I could write about hundreds of thousands of others who were dealt a very hard hand in life but chose to react in a positive manner. They chose not to be a victim and instead, they become a leader and a legend by making a powerful impact on their lives and the lives of others around them. Anyone using freedom of choice to react to any circumstances in a positive way can lead a happy and powerful life.

Is it OK to do bad things?

Bad and good are really the same thing, in that they both describe a measurement to an action seen, heard, or read. Depending on our interpretation of the action, it will be labeled either bad, good, or somewhere in between.

No one does anything bad on purpose, in that no action is carried out with the intention of solely doing something bad. They may feel in their mind that what they are doing is wrong or bad beforehand, but there is some underlying reason why they proceed with a known bad action. Sometimes it's to gain attention to a problem or situation and is a form of crying out for help.

Right and Wrong

What determines if something is right or wrong?

Like beauty, right and wrong is in the eye of the observer. There are really no absolute rights and wrongs, even though there are laws, cultural teachings, religious, and non-religious documents stating certain acts and even thoughts are right and wrong. What is right and wrong is a moving target and can shift, given certain circumstances. What determines whether the resulting consequences from a thought, word, and action is right or wrong is based on what works or doesn't or what is functional or dysfunctional, given what an individual or group is trying to do, accomplish, or achieve at any given moment in time.

How can the same thing be seen as both right and wrong depending upon the observer?

An individual's interpretation of whether something is right or wrong is dependent upon their own belief system. Everyone's belief system determines how things should or should not be, what it is they're trying to do in their life, and the effects those action have on what they want their life to be like. Since we interpret right or wrong based on our belief system, something can easily be interpreted as both right and wrong by two or more observers. So, when we say something is right or wrong, what we're really saying is that something does or does not meet our belief system.

Is a belief system the same as religion?

No, a belief system is not the same thing as religious belief, even though religious convections play a vital part in forming a belief system. The term "belief system" is used because we all have a belief system, regardless of whether we follow a particular religious belief, or if we are atheists or agnostics.

How can we change someone's opinion about what is right or wrong?

To change a person's perception about right or wrong, we must address their belief system.

How is everyone's interpretation of what's right and wrong formed?

Right and wrong are formed through cultural, societal, and belief systems conditioning.

What determines whether something is actually right or wrong?

Societal laws and spiritual laws determine if an action, inaction, spoken words, or unspoken words are right or wrong. Societal laws are manmade and are carried out by our judicial systems.

Spiritual laws are also manmade laws of an organized religion or internal life values of an individual and their conscience.

If societal laws are not broken, then spiritual laws determine if an action is right or wrong. If our value system or conscience tells us a particular action is wrong in a particular context, then it is wrong.

The purpose of this discussion is not to try and judge whether any action is right, wrong, good, or bad but to accept the action as it is, and that there are reasons behind each and every action. Nothing occurs by accident or without reasons. We may not know or understand why something we perceive as bad and wrong occurs, but we must know, through faith, there are reasons.

Why are there so many bad people in the world?

There is no such thing as bad people, only bad decisions made by inherently good people, based on their belief system. The basic nature of humans at birth and during early childhood is to be lovable and to be loved. Humans begin to stray from this birthright as we grow up and are taught by our parents, teachers, religion, and society what to believe, which forms our initial belief system.

I believe the number of individuals labeled as bad people is small. But technological advancements, like TV and the Internet makes it appear there are more bad people in the world than good, simply because these technologies have increased the speed in which news travels, and that news being accessible 24/7. News tends to focus on crimes, warfare, disasters, and other human suffering happening worldwide. That escalates fear and makes it seem we are surrounded by bad people because people know more about what's going on in the world than they did before these technologies.

Why do people make bad decisions?

I believe there is no such thing as a bad decision for the decisionmaker, at the moment in time the decision is made. These decisions are always the right decision to the person making them. I don't believe anyone, at the moment a decision is made, says to themselves: "*I am doing this because it is bad.*" People may know in their heart an action is bad, but they are making a point, trying to get someone's attention, bringing attention to a cause they strongly believe in, reacting to a delusion, etc.

The following is an example of someone doing something known as bad, but based on their belief systems, follows through on their decision. A person has a strong belief that abortion is wrong and decides to burn down an abortion clinic. They know in their heart it is wrong to destroy another person's property, but, at the moment in time of burning the clinic, their belief system is telling them they are saving the fetus' life. After burning the clinic down, it was discovered a cleaning person was in the building at the time of the act and was burned to death.

Another example is when people know it's bad to take illegal drugs, but making the decision to take those drugs may be a cry for help or a means to escape their real problems.

How can stealing, killing, or harming a child be right?

Hideous crimes are very difficult to understand and justify as being an acceptable action. But, at the moment a hideous act is performed, in the mind of the perpetrator, the act can be justified as being the right thing, given the perpetrator's belief system.

As an example, let's say we witnessed one man chasing another down the street. The first man catches up with him, and beats him to death. Our first reaction, based on our belief system is that it was wrong to kill the man being chased down the street. But, if we knew the whole story, we may have a paradigm shift and change our minds.

What we did not know is the man that was killed had broken into the other man's house, thinking no one was home, unexpectedly encountered a mother and her daughter, and killed them in a panic. The robber thought it was right to kill the family because they could identify him and, based on his belief system, if caught, he could not take care of his family while in jail.

The husband came home and saw the horrific scene of his wife and daughter as the man was escaping from the house. The husband began chasing the criminal out the door, caught up with him, and beat him to death, because, based on his belief system, an eye-for-an-eye killing is justified. So, based on this version of the story, we will more than likely change our mind because, based on our belief system, the killing was justified for the same reason as the husband.

The other side of the story is that the robber was breaking into the house in the first place to steal valuables to sell them. The robber was laid off, his child has a potential life-threatening illness, and he was unable to cover the cost of the medical care needed to save his child's life. The robber thought it was the right thing to steal and kill because his belief system was to provide and take care of his family. His only recourse, in his mind, was to steal from someone and sell the goods to cover his child's medical costs.

I am not defending anyone who performs a hideous act and I have great sympathy and compassion toward the victims and those close to the victims. However, I think everyone does what they believe is the right thing to do at that moment in time, based on their belief system.

Is it right to abort a fetus?

The question is not whether the decision to have an abortion is right or wrong, but whether the decision to have an abortion is in alignment with the pregnant woman's belief system. The mother will abort the fetus if her belief systems believes abortions are acceptable. If the mother's belief systems believes abortions are not acceptable, she will not have an abortion and either keep the baby or put it up for adoption.

Many people believe it is totally wrong to abort the life of a fetus. No matter you're your belief, we all need to understand there is a reason why the fetus was aborted and not judge the woman.

One reason for aborting a fetus may be to allow the woman the opportunity to fulfill her purpose in life. She may have decided, prior to being incarnated as a soul, to be a spokesperson about the mental, physical, and emotional aspects before and after an abortion. As mentioned before, we can conceptually understand something but to truly understand, we need to experience it. By the woman deciding to experience an abortion, she will be in the position to truly speak to other pregnant women about the mental, emotional, and physical aspects before and after an abortion.

I am not trying to say an abortion is right or wrong. All I am trying to do is not judge whether the woman's decision is right or wrong to abort a fetus, but understand there is a reason for every decision, even if we don't believe or understand the reason for that decision.

Doesn't the fetus's soul have a say about being aborted or not?

The fetus does have a say. The fetus's spirit decides to be part of the abortion prior to being incarnated as the soul of the fetus. As mentioned in the section about the soul's mission, the spirit decides its purposes or purposes in life prior to being incarnated as a soul in a body. Therefore, the soul of the fetus had its say when it was still a spirit, prior to being incarnated at conception with the fetus.

Why would the soul of the fetus want to be aborted?

Prior to becoming a soul of the fetus, the spirit's only purpose may have been to help a mother who has decided to have an abortion, to help others understand the emotions and feelings of an abortion.

What makes abortion such an emotional and controversial topic is many people rightfully feel sorry for the fetus losing its life. One way to help ease the emotional pain is to believe it was the fetus's purpose in life to be aborted. Another way to ease the emotional pain is understanding more about what happens after death. One of the options after death is for the fetus's soul to come back and be incarnated back in the mother's womb, so instead of taking the path to being aborted, take the path of being born. Everything that can happen happens within the space-time continuum, and in this case, the path of not being aborted is taken.

Does a spirit decide who its parents are going to be?

Yes. For those who had an extremely difficult and painful childhood, the answer to this question may be very hard to accept. I'm not making excuses for abusive parents, but there is a reason why the parents were abusive to their child and reasons why a spirit chose to experience an abusive childhood. One obvious reason is to be an advocate against child abuse, to help others understand the issue without having to experience it in a future lifetime.

Once again, I am not making excuses for abusive parents and feel strongly they must face the consequences of their actions based on our judicial system.

Is it ever right to kill another human?

The killing of another person is only justified in the eye of the perpetrator, and the killing is based on their belief system.

Why would someone's belief system allow someone to kill another?

An abbreviated list includes the following:

- To save their own life.

- A person may kill another person of another race because their belief system teaches it is acceptable.

- People may kill people of another culture because of fear that their way of life is threaten.

- People may kill people of other countries because they have what the killers want and will contrive reasons in their belief system to attack and kill them.

- People may kill another because their religion tells them to kill those who do not believe in their religion.

The list can go on, but the point is killing of another is understandable by the killer if it meets the purpose of the killer's belief system. Therefore, to stop people from killing each other, we must change their belief systems.

If actions only fulfill one's belief system, why do people go to jail for their actions?

Because society has passed laws determining what actions are illegal.

If there are no wrong decisions, can we do anything and everything we want?

Everyone has freedom of choice and can do anything they want. However, with every action, there is a reaction and for every decision, there are consequences. The consequences can be considered favorable or unfavorable, depending upon whether societal and/or spiritual laws are broken.

How can we only make right decisions and end up living in poverty?

There is a soul purpose for the impoverished life. We can't judge the impoverished life as being right or wrong because we do not know what the soul's or spirit's purpose for the person impoverished. Everyone's condition and lifestyle, at every moment in time, has been created by the decisions made during their lifetime, and those have been the right decisions for them, based on the purpose of their soul and/or spirit.

The following is a true story, which was made into the song "Ode to Jake," by George Ensle from Austin, TX. A boy in Syracuse, NY, decided to play hooky from school on a wintry day. He was walking across an iced-over bridge that did not have a railing. He slipped on the icy road and fell onto the frozen pond below. He fell through the ice and down to the bottom of the pond, but was able to push off the bottom of the river back up to the hole in the ice. He was struggling to keep his head above the water and each time he tried to grab the ice, it would break away. Now, when the boy was near exhaustion and the cold water was about to take him under, a homeless man living under the bridge in a makeshift hut was awakened from a drunken stupor by the boy's cry for help. The man was able to pull the boy from the water and save his life.

We can easily assume that most people would say the homeless person had probably made numerous wrong decisions throughout his life to end up as a homeless drunk living under a bridge. However, had he made the so-called right decisions in life, he would not have been living under that bridge at that moment in time to save that boy's life.

The point is not to judge other people's lives as being good, bad, right, or wrong because we don't know what their purpose in life is. There is no such thing as a wasted life.

What about children born into extreme poverty?

The unbearable suffering children born into the poorest of countries must endure is very difficult to understand as being the purpose of their lives. One possible purpose is to awaken humanity's eyes to such conditions and the atrocities committed against children and their mothers, so it can be stopped, thus enabling those souls and/or spirits to meet their purpose in life of healing or providing a service.

What if we break God's law?

God has no laws. God gave us the greatest gift, the freedom of choice to do whatever we want. Why would God create laws and boundaries to prevent our spirit from experiencing all that was created by God while incarnated as and in human form?

Doesn't God send people to Hell if God's laws are broken?

First, the supposed laws of God are not God's laws but spiritual laws created by religious organizations in the name of God. I don't believe there is such a thing as Hell in God's creation. It was created by certain religious leaders to keep people obeying their religion's doctrine through fear. If we disobeyed, God would send us to Hell, not Heaven.

Religions creating a fictitious Hell in the afterlife caused fear, psychological scars, and phobias while on Earth. Many wars and social conflicts can be traced back to religions and their belief systems.

Did Genghis Khan and Hitler go to Heaven?

Yes. My belief will be very hard for most people reading this book to understand and comprehend. I'm not saying I approve of mass killings; I'm just saying, in my belief system, those leaders and their followers who carried out the killings went to Heaven because there is no other place to go. Since I don't believe Hell exists, Heaven is the only place they can go.

I believe we all go to Heaven because God is the beautiful, ultimate example of unconditional love and total forgiveness, no matter what we may say or do. God created us to experience all It knows conceptually and gave us the freedom of choice, so why would God condemn us for something It gave us?

I see God as the mother/father of humankind. I'm a father and there is no action, no matter how hideous, that would cause me to stop loving my son for who he was, not what he became. I would be sad and disappointed, yes, but no, I would not want him condemned to a place of everlasting torture. I would condemn him to a place of everlasting love and joy. I would accept the consequences of societal laws but would still go to see him wherever the laws of the land sent him and tell him I still love him for who he was. If a human being can love and forgive, it is no small leap to think God can certainly do the same.

DECISION MAKING

How do we know when we're making the right decisions during our lifetime?

We always make the right decision or choice. All choices and decisions, at the moment in time the choice or decision is made, are the right choices because nobody makes a choice or decision knowing it is the wrong decision or choice. If someone does make a decision or choice and knows it is wrong, it's a cry for help or the person's belief system deems it the right thing to do.

Why do I sometimes have a hard time deciding or procrastinate?

Most people have a hard time deciding because they are afraid of making the wrong decision. But I believe there is no such thing as a wrong decision at the moment in time the decision is made. If we believe and understand that whatever the decision made is the right decision, it is easier to make a decision. I see three phases to the decision-making process.

The first is gathering as much information as possible from our area of influence to make the best decision at that moment in time. The influence arena consists of three areas of input—internal, external, and soul.

Internal consist of input from the mind, based on one's past life experiences. If we are making a decision that is like one made in the past, recall the consequences from the school of hard knocks and apply it to the next decision.

External consists of input from social cultural conditioning, belief system cultural conditioning, and family and friends, who can provide us feedback that can only be seen from looking in from the outside to see how it can affect us.

The soul's input involves listening to the feelings and thoughts experienced when considering the decision.

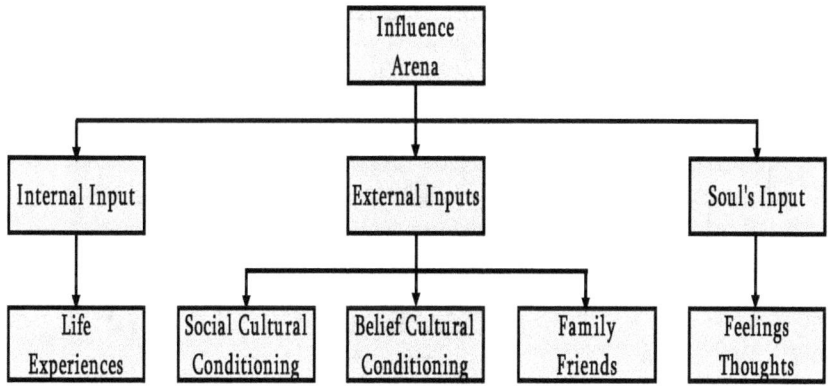

The information gathered from each arena does not take very long. However, the time involved with gathering information determines the seriousness of the decision. We can take our time but also avoid paralysis from over analyzing. We do not have to be afraid to make an informed decision since all decisions, in the moment they are made, are the right decisions.

After the gathering the internal, external, and soul's input, the next step is to make a sound decision based on the information gathered. At this stage, we have gathered and thought of all we can. It is key that we do not beat ourselves up later if we did not think of everything.

During this phase, it is very important to find a place of peace so we can be out of our mind and away from our ego. When the decision is totally based on ego, the mind shuts off all emotions and feelings. We want a decision based on the truth spoken from our heart.

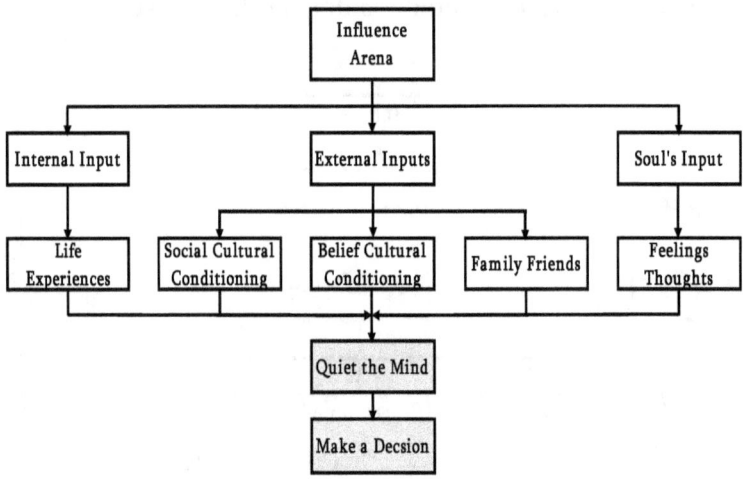

Once a decision is made by the mind, the body acts out the decision. The next phase is to observe the results of the decision based on the consequences. The process is a classic example of the freedom of choice we all have by using our body, mind, and soul. I see it as the creative process of thought, word, and action, in which the thought is the gathering process, word is deciding, and action is the body acting out the decision.

What happens after the consequences are known?

The consequences of the decision are the cumulative input and effects of spiritual laws - (if our belief system has them) -

physical laws of nature, societal laws, and the reaction by us and the people involved with the issue.

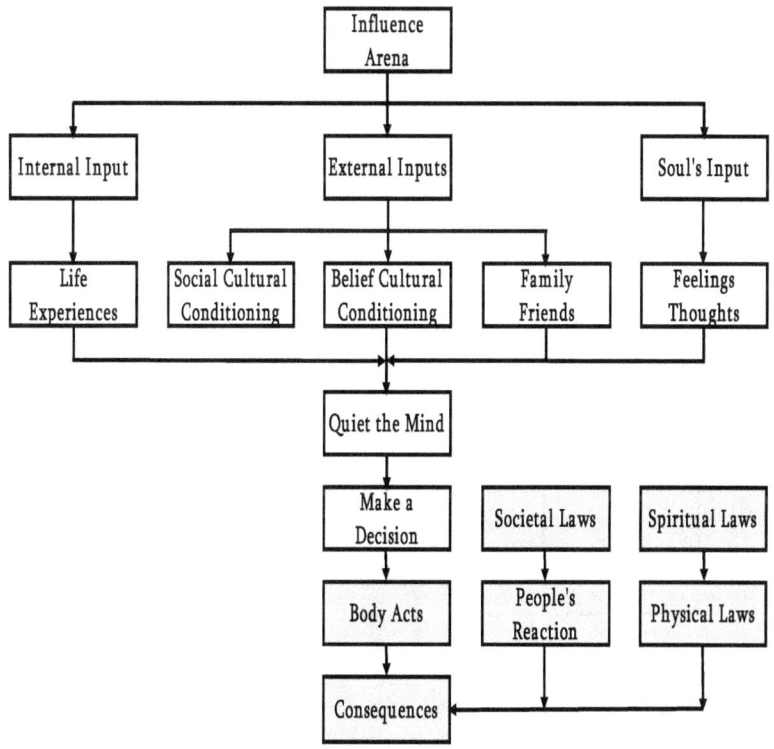

If the results are favorable, then the decision was the right choice at the moment in time the decision was made. If the results were not favorable, the wrong decision was not made, but the right choice at the moment in time the decision was made, just with unfavorable consequences.

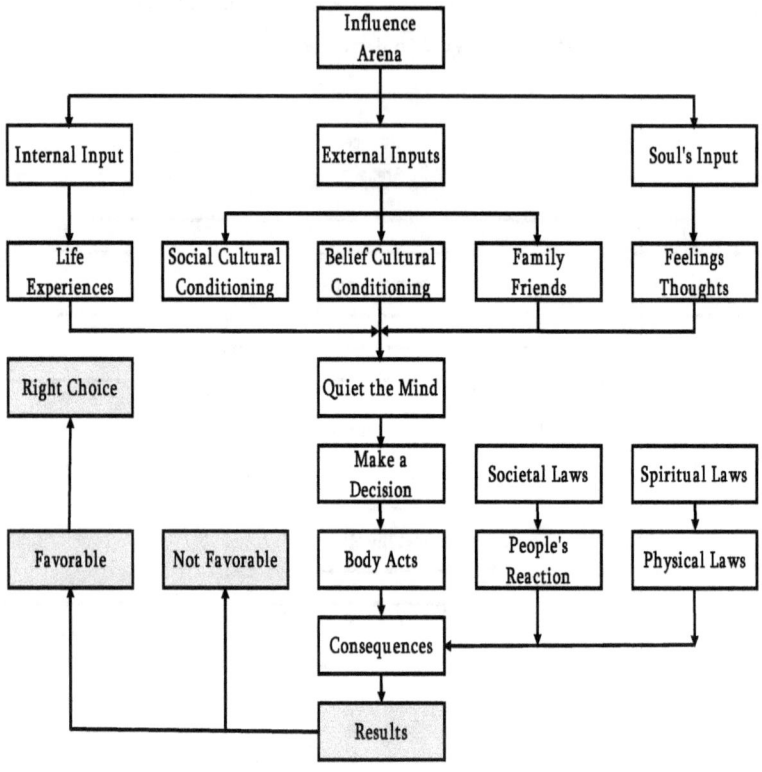

How can a choice that was not favorable become the right choice?

If any decision turns out not to be favorable, it becomes a learning experience from the school of hard knocks and a valuable lesson taught and learned. The other reason it becomes the right choice is that we are able to catalog it into our library of social cultural conditioning of the external input influence arena and use the experience the next moment in time a decision or choice is made.

Are all decisions and choices ultimately the right choice no matter the consequences?

I believe they are because there is a lesson to be learned from all choices and decisions made at the moment in time the decision is made, regardless the consequences. If the consequences were negative, but resulted in something learned that can prevent the same person or others from making the same wrong choice, then it can be seen as the right choice.

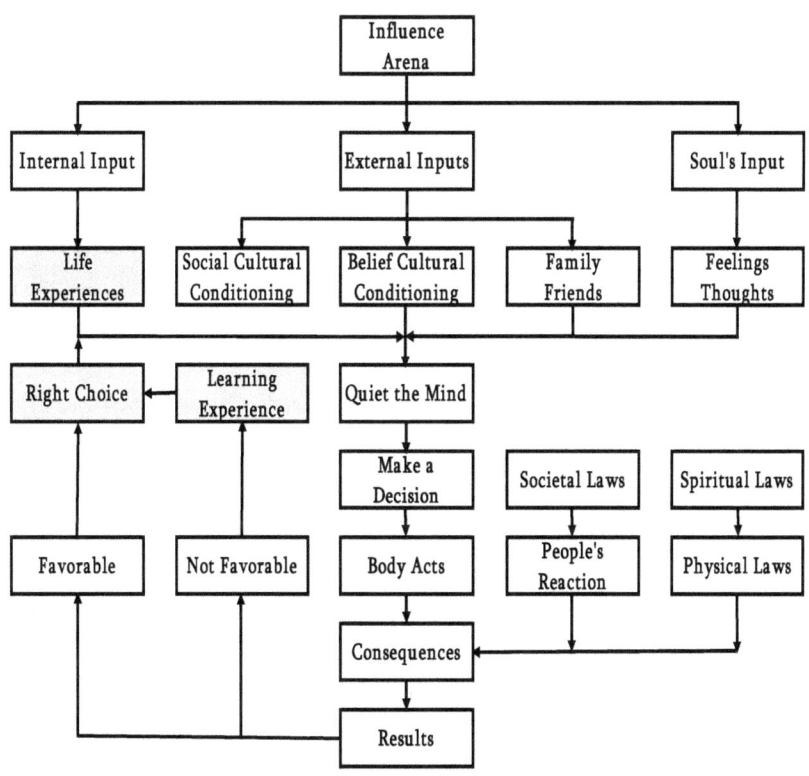

What about when a quick decision is needed?

The decision-making process, as described above, can take time, depending upon the seriousness of the decision and how much time is involved in making the decision. There is an abbreviated version that will come in handy when needing to make quick decision. When deciding, no matter if it is the long version or this short version, it is key to make the choice that represents love, not fear.

Which decisions represent love and which are represented by fear?

A decision that is represented by love is one that draws us closer in a healthy way to another being, whether human, animal, or plant. A loving choice heals past wounds, releases fears and anxieties, amends past actions, shares the truth and kindness of our heart, allows us to grow emotionally, and represents the level of integrity we are striving for. Most all love-based decisions are those made from within after filtering out all the fear-based external inputs.

A decision that is represented by fear is one that creates an unhealthy emotional distance between a person and others. A fear-based choice maintains negative unhealthy aspects of our lives, preventing us from becoming who and what we want to be and draws we away from love. Many of the fear-based decisions come from not understanding fear, as well as those social and belief system cultural conditioning issues that need to be upgraded.

SELFISHNESS

Shouldn't all decisions be unselfish decisions?

No, there are times when it is necessary to make selfish decisions. There are two types of selfish decisions: unhealthy and healthy.

What is healthy selfishness?

Healthy selfishness is making choices and decisions based on what serves or does not serve us, based on our belief system. Based on my belief system, healthy selfishness simply means we do not neglect ourselves to help or please others at the expense of negatively impacting our life and well-being. Healthy selfishness is a form of self-love or self-care, which promotes a happy lifestyle. Healthy selfishness is not giving from the mind but from the heart, which actually feels good and makes us feel open and connected to the person to whom we are giving. We are at our best when we are giving of ourselves from the heart and not from the mind.

The good news is, we will be better equipped to give our love and support unselfishly to others. Healthy selfishness does not mean we do not care about or neglect other people's needs, feelings, or ask for help; it means we cannot be of maximum benefit to them at the present moment in time. Healthy selfishness is optimal for everyone and benefits both the giver and the receiver, whereas unhealthy selfishness is not beneficial to the giver and may or may not benefit the receiver.

What is unhealthy selfishness?

Unhealthy selfishness is living our lives by making the choices and decisions that are not necessarily based on or in alignment with our belief system. Based on my belief system, practicing unhealthy selfishness means we have to be there for others and do whatever it takes, even though our actions have a negative impact financially, mentally, or are a drain on our life energy. Some of the feelings and emotions felt related to unhealthy selfishness include,

- Discomfort at saying no to a loved one.

- Reluctance to say yes to things we really do not want to do.

- Worrying more about other people's needs more than our own.

- Going the extra mile and running ourselves down trying to be there for others.

Unhealthy selfish choices and decisions over an extended period can easily lead to exhaustion, anxiety, and unhappiness, which do not benefit the giver or receiver.

I have found there is a gray area of unhealthy selfishness we all need to be aware of. This gray area is a place where we think we do not have the mental or financial ability yet, at the same time, we feel we can help and be there for another. The times I thought about and rationalized the decision and helped, I found it was not beneficial for me or the receiver. The times when I was in the gray area and made my decision from the heart, I found that not only was it of help to the receiver but also increased my life energy.

What causes us to make unhealthy selfish decisions and choices?

Primarily fear.

How are unhealthy selfish decisions and choices tied into fear?

Many people have been taught to believe it is wrong to be selfish and, as a result, the fear being labeled as selfish becomes prevalent in their lives. The fear of being selfish asserts one has to be there for others whenever they need us and do whatever it takes, even if it has a negative impact on one's own mental well-being, personal life, and family life. Unhealthy selfish choices and decisions also occur when fear acts as a demotivator.

How can fear act as a demotivator?

Fear can also be tied to selflessness when fear is the demotivator or excuse for not fulfilling our purpose in life as a messenger, teacher, or in helping others. Our superconscious plants a seed in our conscious in an attempt to move us toward being a messenger, teacher, or in helping others. What can happen is, instead of cultivating these seeds of purpose, fearful thoughts fill our consciousness. Sampling of such fearful thoughts are,

- What will people think if I fail.
- What if I look like a fool.
- What if I lose credibility.
- I will be judged.
- I will be rejected.

- I can't do this it will take too much work, etc.

A typical definition of selfishness is caring only for one's own interests, thoughts, feelings, benefits, and welfare, regardless of others. When fearful thoughts enter our consciousness, we are thinking of our own feelings and interests, regardless of whether they may be of benefit or help to others. As an example, let's assume our purpose in life is to be a messenger or teacher and a seed is planted in our consciousness by our superconscious to write a book. The initial excitement is our superconscious speaking to us through feelings from the heart. Then, our logical conscious mind begins creating the fearful thoughts of, "*What if they dislike what I have to say,*" "*What if I fail and I am ridiculed,*" "*People will not believe what I am saying,*" etc. What can unfortunately happen is our selfish act, created by the fear of what others may think, prevents us from writing the book that will help others. This is an unhealthy selfish act. We all can think of a time when fear became a demotivator in preventing us from following through on a dream or a powerful and motivating love-based thought.

What can I do to make love-based decisions?

Given that all decisions are either based on fear or love, if fear is not part of the decision-making process, then all decisions will be based on love. Unfortunately, fear is part of everyone's decision-making process. Fear is created when we feel or think there is a need for something we may lose or be without. When faced with fear, take a close look at what need is creating the fear. I believe I have control over my fears because I am the source of my fears. I overcome those fears by facing the need with a spirit of excitement and knowing they are not real. No matter the consequences of a decision, I'll be the wiser for it and live to see another day. A life without fear is a life of without need, and a life without need is a life full of love, peace, and happiness.

Secondly, I consider what my upgraded social and belief systems tells me is a love-based decision. Thirdly and most important, I go to my place of peace and listen to that quiet whisper of my feelings and emotions spoken from the heart. I truly feel if we practice love-based healthy selfishness from now until the day we die, we will have lived a rewarding, happy, and fulfilling life.

FORGIVENESS

What is the definition of forgiveness?

There are two levels of forgiveness: forgiveness toward the act and forgiveness toward the perpetrator. My definition of forgiveness toward a malicious and senseless act is the conscious and deliberate decision to internally release feelings of sadness, loss, and sorrow. Forgiveness toward the perpetrator is the conscious and deliberate decision to internally release feelings of hatred, anger, revenge, and vengeance toward the perpetrator.

When is it possible to forgive the perpetrator of the malicious and harmful act?

I believe there are certain unreasonable malicious senseless acts which create such intense, unbearable, lasting physical or mental pain that it makes it impossible to completely forgive the perpetrator. What is considered a senseless act varies from individual to individual. For me, senseless acts include the meaningless killing of our daughter, son, spouse, close family member, loved ones, friends, or mass killings for some obscure needless purpose, etc.

Isn't it wrong not to forgive someone?

No, it is not wrong to forgive the perpetrator. However, holding onto the feelings of sadness, loss, and sorrow toward the act can be extremely harmful to our physical and mental well-being.

How can we move on with our lives without forgiving perpetrators of pain?

In order to move on with our lives without forgiving the perpetrator, one must arrive at a state of release. A state of release brings finality to the act (not the perpetrator) to the point we are no longer bound to sadness, loss, and sorrow, but released and allowed to function normally and effectively from one day to the next. Keep in mind, reaching a state of release does not mean we deny or minimize the seriousness of the act, forget, condone, pardon, or release the perpetrator from being accountable for their actions.

Why is it important to reach a state of release?

By not arriving at a state of release, our mind and bodies will eventually experience a higher and higher levels of physical illness and mental instability. The state of release will bring a level of closure of the act to a point where we can move forward with our lives in a healthy way and help prevent anger, hatred, and thoughts of revenge from consuming the remainder of our lives.

How does one achieve a state of release?

One achieves a state of release by finding ways to let go of the sadness, loss, and sorrow in a non-physical, non-violent manner. The following are samples of ways to begin the journey toward a state of release.

- Allow yourself time for your mind to face and work through the anger and hatred. When the time is right, quiet our mind, go to your place of peace and begin a dialogue with your internal voice, which speaks from the heart. During this time, have a pencil and pad (not a computer) and manually write out your negative feeling and hateful thoughts, as if you are writing to the perpetrator. Next, attempt to place yourself in their position and try to understand their purpose for their harmful act. Unless the perpetrator is mentally ill, they are not void of thoughts and feelings and have a reason or purpose for their actions. Unless someone is trying to draw attention to themselves or a specific cause, a perpetrator will not follow through on an act with the thought of, *"I am doing this because it is bad."* I believe a person is born incapable of evil intents, but through their cultural conditioning become capable of acting out maliciously. I am not trying to make excuses or condone any evil and malicious act but, by attempting to put ourselves in their shoes, it brings a certain level of "why" toward the act to help you reach a point of finality and release. Reaching a state of release from the harmful and painful act is, for you, not the perpetrator, and by having a hint of compassion and understanding of "why," helps you move forward to a state of release. Once finished writing, symbolically and emotionally release the anger, resentment, and vengeance by burning the paper.

- Find a therapist, psychologist, or psychiatrist that specializes in forgiveness.

- Join a support group recommended by the therapist that includes others struggling to move forward with their lives after a tragic event.

- If the senseless act has an organization dedicated towards preventing the same or similar senseless acts from occurring again, join the organization and become active within the group.

As a reminder, reaching a state of release is a gradual process; it is not a quick, overnight fix, does not let the perpetrator "off the hook," and will not erase the event from our minds but will allow us to move on with our lives in a healthy manner. Reaching a state of release will put a final stamp on the act so we are no longer bound to it in a negative way, but we will be better equipped to take care of ourselves mentally and physically from one day to the next.

How can there be a possible reason or purpose for someone acting out a malicious and harmful act?

As hard as it is to believe, there is a reason and or purpose for every action, including malicious and harmful acts. I believe there is no such thing as a malicious and harmful act at the moment in time the decision is made; these decisions are always the right decision to the perpetrator. I don't believe anyone at the moment a decision is made says to themselves: *"I am doing this because it is a malicious or harmful act."* People may know in their heart an action is malicious and harmful, but they are making a point, trying to get someone's attention, bringing attention to a cause they strongly believe in, etc. It is important to understand there is a reason or purpose behind each and every harmful and malicious act. Nothing occurs by accident or without reason. We may not know or understand why a malicious and harmful act occurs, but we must know, through faith in our belief system, there is a purpose and reason.

How is it possible to forgive the perpetrator of the malicious and harmful act?

Forgiving the harmful act is dependent upon the actions taken by the one harmed, whereas the perpetrator must earn forgiveness. In order for the perpetrator to be considered as being forgiven, their future actions must create the possibility of putting themselves in a place of being forgiven.

How does the perpetrator of a harmful act arrive at a place of being forgiven?

The perpetrator of the harmful act must begin the process of being forgiven by first announcing sincere regret for their actions and taking complete ownership and responsibility of their actions, **without** rationalization, justification, or excuses. Words alone are not enough, thus the perpetrator must show they have taken ownership and responsibility, through sincere action over an extended period of time. Sincere actions over time will exhibit remorse over their actions and show a true desire to make amends. Once the perpetrator has placed themselves in a place of being forgiven, it is up to the ones harmed to forgive the perpetrator.

Why does God allow malicious and harmful acts to occur?

God is the creator of all there is and all that can happen (including malicious and harmful acts) within the space-time continuum, but God is not responsible for human's decisions to execute malicious and harmful acts within it. Humans make these decisions through God's gift of freedom of choice in order for the human's spirit to experience its reason and purpose on Earth.

DEATH AND DYING

What is death and what happens when we die?

Death occurs when our physical body and mind cease to exist. At the movement of death, our soul is released back into the afterlife as a spirit once again.

Does our spirit ever die?

The spirit never dies; it is in a continuous cycle of being created anew from one lifetime to the next.

Who decides the time of our death?

It is either our minds (consciousness) or our souls/spirits (superconsciousness) that decide the time of death. God does not personally decide the time of our death but, given we are pieces of God, it is these pieces (superconscious) of God that decide.

When the mind (consciousness) decides its time to die, it is called suicide. When the mind feels all hope is lost, it turns to suicide to escape the emotional, spiritual, and physical loneliness and ends life prior to experiencing its purpose in life.

Isn't it wrong to commit suicide and won't we go to Hell?

I don't believe there is a Hell that consists of everlasting torture, fire, and brimstone, as described in certain religions. And as earlier explained, I don't believe there are wrong decisions.

If the suicide prevents the soul/spirit from experiencing what it was sent to Earth to experience, then the soul/spirit is returned back to the space-time continuum prior to the moment of committing suicide and takes the path on the space-time continuum of not committing suicide.

What about medical-assisted death and euthanasia?

If the death from euthanasia occurred before the soul/spirit has experienced what it set out to do on Earth, it would follow the same process as if someone who committed suicide. If the spirit/soul has fulfilled its life experience before being euthanized, or if being euthanized is the spirit/soul's message to the world, then it will follow each phase of death as of those who have experienced their life experiences.

When does the superconscious (soul/spirit) decide when to die?

The superconscious decides the time of death when all of the experiences, reasons, and purpose for incarnating as soul have been completed. I also think, on rare occasions, the soul/spirit decides to die when it becomes frustrated with the mind not making the decisions in alignment with its purpose on Earth. When this occurs, the soul/spirit commits a temporary spiritual suicide and takes a break. After the break, it returns to the point in time prior to committing spiritual suicide in hopes of the mind doing a better job at making decisions in alignment with its purpose on Earth. The soul/spirits enlist the help of other soul/spirits to help the person's mind make better decisions.

Who decides the time of death in accidents and natural disasters?

If, at the time of death, the soul/spirit has completed its experience and purpose of life, it is the soul/spirt that decides the time of death and proceeds through the death phases.

Why is it important to understand death?

Once we understand death, we can live life fully, in peace, without fear, and have a graceful and peaceful departure from the physical plane of Earth. We can then begin the next life experience. Death is designed to move forward to the next lifetime experience and not be an escape from something. Understand that the sacredness of the physical life and death we experience after fulfilling the experiences on Earth in alignment with the soul's purpose is of unspeakable spiritual proportions.

Could I live a life of peace if I don't understand death?

I could live a life of peace for most of my life without addressing the issue of death but the time came when I had to ask myself: "*What happens when I die?*"

What happens if someone never understands death?

I think people can live their entire lives without coming to grips with death and that's acceptable. But when approaching death, there will be a feeling of uneasiness, doubt, and fear. The good news is, it does not matter; all spirits go through the same stages of death.

Why is there so much sadness and grief over the passing of a loved one?

The sadness and grief are our way to honor the loved one who has passed on to the afterlife. I believe the one who has passed on will be able to see our grief and sadness and will feel touched and honored, knowing they were part of a special, timeless, and precious relationship.

The death of the body and mind, and the moving of one's spirit back to the afterlife, is the single greatest event of one's lifetime, but, for the loved ones left behind, it is a time of unmeasurable sadness and grief that is a measuring stick for how close or strong the relationship was, be it with family, friend, or a spouse.

Over time, the grief and sadness will be replaced by the memories, good times, and undying love that formed the foundation of the relationship.

What happens when we die?

There are five phases for both the believers and non-believers to experience: freedom, afterlife, meet with God, Heaven, and communion.

Phase 1, freedom, begins after the body dies and the mind and spirit are freed. Phase 1 is the same for everyone, regardless of the belief systems. Initially, the conscious (mind) and superconscious (spirit) are uncertain on what has happened, but will eventually realize they are no longer part of their body.

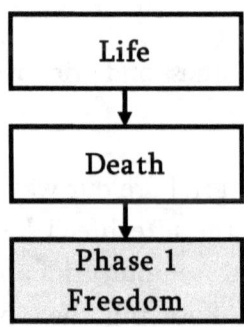

Nonbelievers (atheists and agnostics) and those believers who felt their life was a failure or that nobody cared about them, go directly to Phase 2.

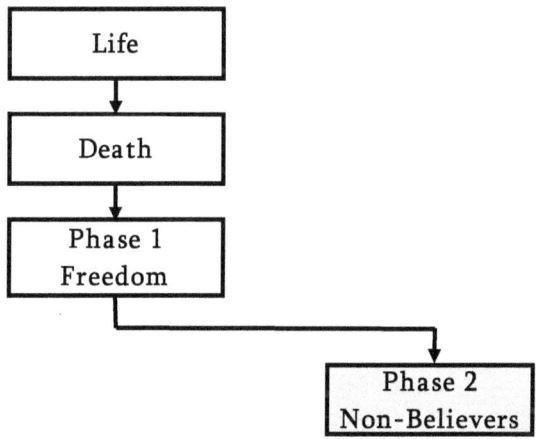

Believers linger in Phase 1. They are those who had family and friends who loved them and felt their life had meaning. They are still part of the earthly experience and have the ability to be at other locations to see and be with family and loved ones on Earth. There will come a time of acceptance of physical death and comfort knowing family and friends will be alright. Phase 1 ends when the mind dies and we only exist as a spirit and no longer are the soul of the human body-mind experience.

In Phase 2, the spirit of nonbelievers in the afterlife will experience exactly what they believe occurs after death—nothingness. Their experience of nothingness will be similar to sleeping with no dreams: only darkness and no thoughts or awareness. Eventually, the nonbeliever will slowly and gently wake up, in limbo between consciousness and sleep. I imagine after awakening, there is a feeling of confusion, uncertainty, and a level of fear of what is happening but slowly, these feelings fade as the nonbeliever is slowly and carefully surrounded by the spirits of deceased family members and loved ones they trusted while alive. Perhaps only one spirit shows up, someone they were closest to while both were alive on Earth.

In due time, with all the love and patience of their loved ones, the nonbelievers eventually realize they can create their own afterlife. God is not present during this process, but the feeling of God—a warm, soft bathing light emitting a feeling of total acceptance and unconditional love—will be there. Then the nonbeliever will begin to experience Phase 2.

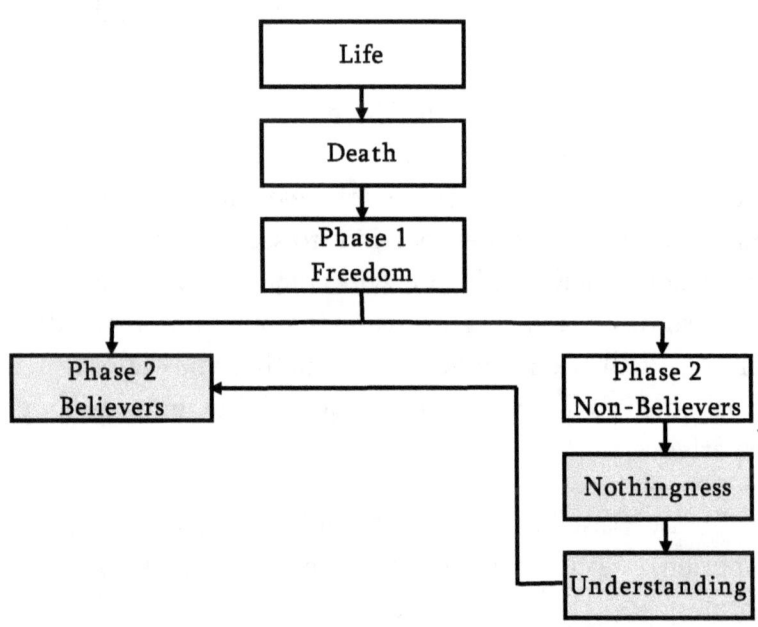

If one has fulfilled its purpose in life, can the spirit go back and visit loved ones?

Yes, there are many ways a spirit can go back and visit loved ones. Some examples are by returning in a dream, as a mental voice in the mind of a loved one, by creating a feeling of a presence that reassures the living our spirit is near, or by creating a vison.

I believe that once we are a spirit again, we can see or be with our loved one left behind just by thinking about seeing them. In the spiritual realm, spirits are formless with no mass, so they can travel at the speed of thought and reach the loved one instantly.

The toughest part of death is the sadness and sorrow experienced by the loved ones left behind. I believe the departed spirit can be there with anyone just by thinking about them. So, I advise people to go ahead and talk to them; they will always be available to listen and, if possible, might respond as a mental voice.

For those left behind, be thankful for the pain and sorrow, because it is a yardstick for measuring how blessed and wonderful our life with the departed was. Odd as it may sound, the better our life was with the departed, the greater the pain and sorrow. The good news for those left behind is knowing the departed can be with us in spirit at any time, and the belief we will see them and be together once again.

What happens during Phase 2 for believers?

I believe believers who commit suicide prevent the soul/spirit from experiencing what it was sent to Earth to experience, then the soul/spirit is returned back to the space-time continuum prior to the moment of committing suicide and takes the path on the space-time continuum of not committing suicide.

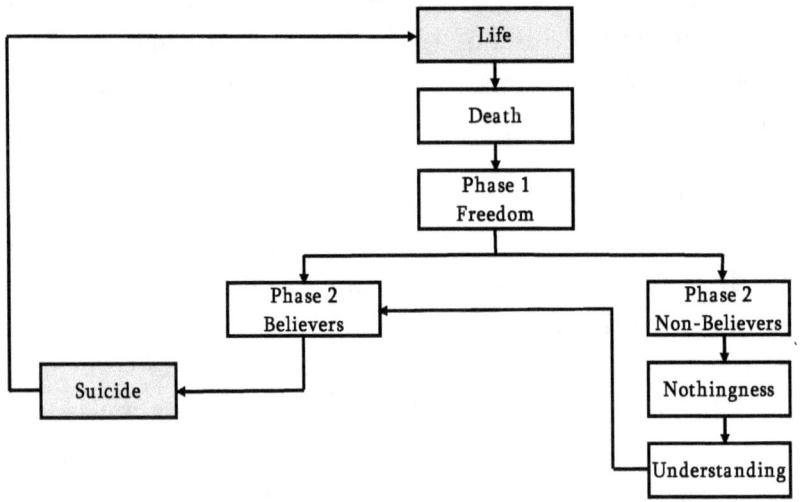

I believe believers who did not commit suicide enter into the greeting room of the spiritual realm, which surrounds the spirit with an array of colors and is filled with the most pleasant and calming musical-like humming, unlike anything heard on Earth, which totally puts our spirit at ease.

The Greatest Mysteries of Life and Beyond Life

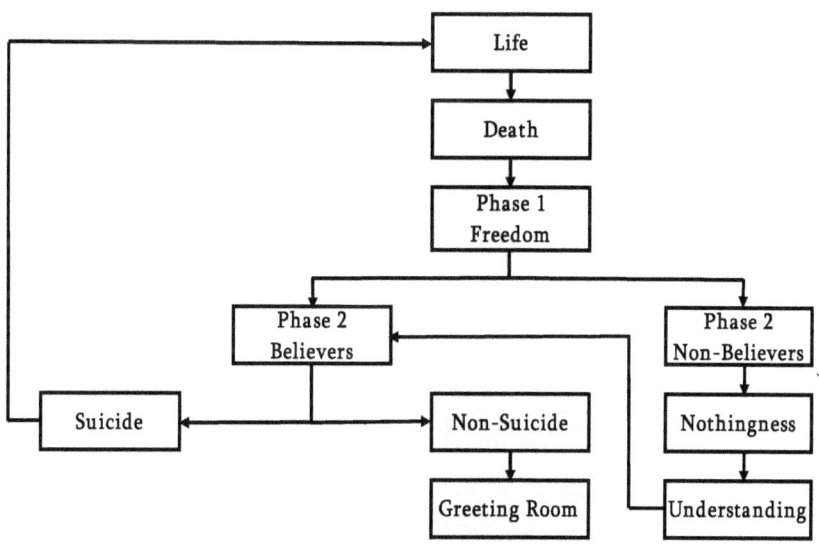

In the greeting room, there will be a party where we are the main attraction and in attendance will be the spirits of family members, friends, loved ones, and yes, pets. Even though they are spirits, we will be able recognize each one of them because their spirits will take the visual form of how we best remember them. There will also be spirits of people we have never met, whose lives we profoundly and meaningfully impacted by thoughts, words, or action while on Earth and did not know about. It will be a reunion beyond our imagination.

After this joyous meeting we meet with God. The ever-present warm, soft light that engulfs the spirit during Phase 2 forms a long, open light chamber leading to another part of the spiritual realm. The spirit is automatically drawn through the chamber toward a bright light, which is the entry point into the spiritual realm of the space-time continuum where God lives. The moment of entering the spiritual realm of God's home is the rebirth of our spirit. When I think of the long chamber, I imagine spirits drawn through, as a birth canal, to be reborn again as a spirit. During the journey through the chamber and upon entering God's home, there is no fear or apprehension but total bliss in the ultimate form of peace, joy, and unconditional love.

As we float through the front door of God's home, we will be greeted and welcomed by God in the form of an awe-inspiring brilliant light radiating a form of love that is indescribable. This brilliant light is the spirit of God and at this time, our spirit that is a piece of God has returned back home, where it left prior to becoming a soul of a human.

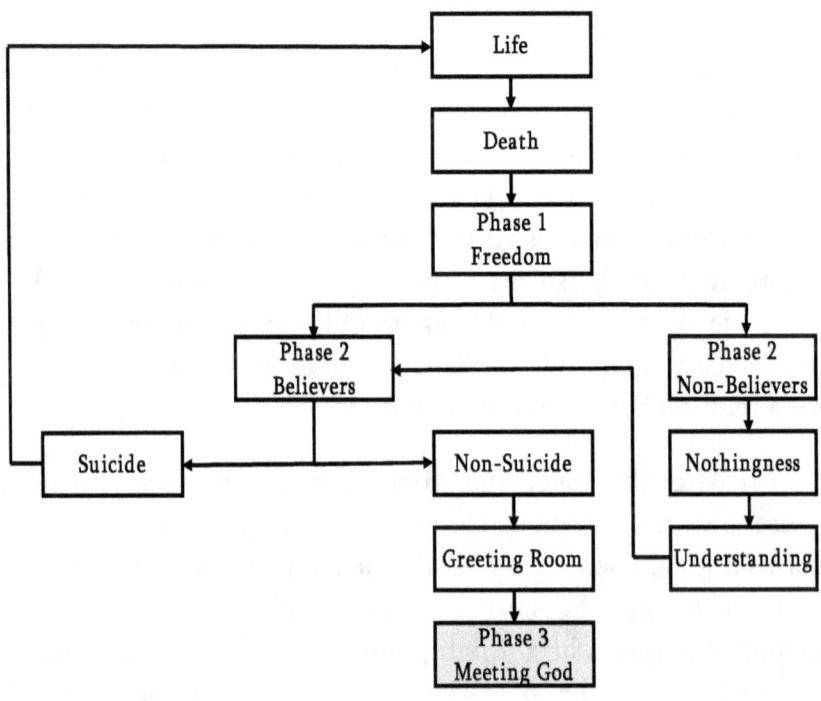

Is God just a light or does God have a physical form?

I believe God's natural state is formless and a light but can become any form It, or we, wishes It to be. If our belief system portrayed God as a wise, elderly man with a long, gray beard and hair, then God will appear in that form to make us as comfortable as possible. We and God will leave the spiritual realm and go as spirits to the physical world of Earth in the space-time continuum, to watch three viewings from our life in live time. This is possible because everything that has happen, is happening, and will happen is occurring all at once in the space-time continuum.

In my vision of what happens, the first viewing is an autobiography of our life, from the time of conception until the time of our body and mind's death, so God can experience what It knows experientially through us, and for our spirit to re-experience and re-feel the consequences of our choices and decisions as a soul/spirit while on Earth. Every thought, deed, and action, the good, bad, and ugly is totally absorbed by our spirit and God. After total immersion with God and transference of all experiences, the spirit is left with an indescribable feeling of beautiful emptiness and peace. At no time during this time of transference does the spirit feel judged by God, ashamed, embarrassed, or sad of its life experiences.

What replaces the beautiful emptiness left after the viewing of our spirit's life experiences is God's unlimited unconditional love, compassion, and understanding. The spirit immediately feels embraced, cherished, nurtured, treasured, protected, understood, and totally at peace with God and itself.

The second viewing is about our life's impact. It's a rerun of the first viewing but, this time, concentrating on how our decisions and choices impacted others, both in a positive and negative way at that moment and in the long term.

By experiencing what other people experienced and felt as a result of our actions, I believe we will be amazed at how the simplest, seemingly benign thought, word, or action can have a profound positive and negative far-reaching effect on so many people for several generations to come. This life review movie ultimately gives us a total picture of our life at every moment in time, and we'll find that the results are often not what we assumed they were.

Viewing this movie will confirm whether I have met my soul/spirit's mission, which may not be to just experience something but to also be a messenger for some issues that need to be addressed or overcome to help humanity constructively move forward from a local and worldwide perspective.

Why is it important to see both movie viewings?

The importance, to me, of viewing these two movies will be to confirm if my life fulfilled the purpose of my soul/spirit's mission while incarnated with the human body.

What happens if, after viewing both movies, my life's purpose(s) was not fulfilled?

If my life's purpose(s) isn't fulfilled, I'll have the opportunity to return to my life in the space-time continuum before I died or go to Heaven. If I decide to return to my life on

Earth, I'll return to my body at a moment in time on the continuum prior to my death.

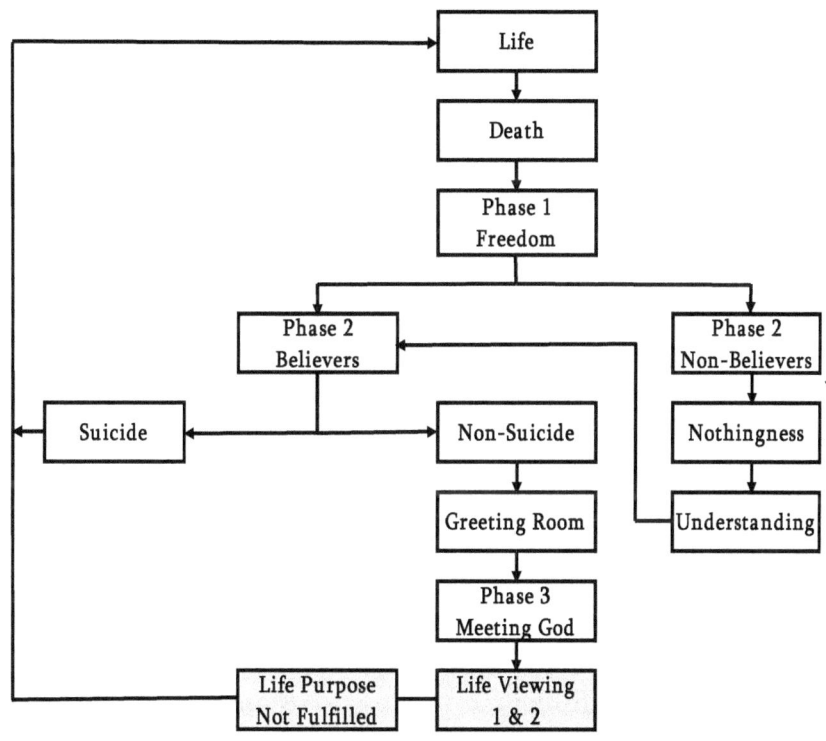

I believe spirits typically return to the body/mind while sleeping prior to the day of a person's death and prevents that death from happening. I won't be surprised when viewing the movie to discover I had died and come back before, especially if I had led a risky or dangerous lifestyle.

Have we ever wondered why we may have done something or how some seemingly minor event changed our path? Have we ever made a turn while driving then wondered why because we had never taken that route? That could have occurred on the day of our death. Had we not turned, it could have ended in a fatal car crash. That unexpected turn allowed us to avoid the life-ending accident and continue with our life to fulfill our purpose.

This turn was set up by our spirit, or with help from other spirits, so we could avoid being killed. If we happen, for some reason, to ignore the messages from our spirit and die again, the same process is repeated until we make the turn.

Can I kill myself to avoid something and then return to avoid it?

In this scenario, we will be able to return to our life but, because we committed suicide, the whole point of returning will be to face it; we won't return to avoid facing something.

My soulmate died; why haven't they come back to me?

The simple but painful response to this question is our soulmate has not returned because they fulfilled their purpose in life or they are fulfilling our purpose to experience the death. To help ease the pain, know that, by thinking of them or calling their name, they will instantly engulf our body with its spirit to listen to us. Don't be shy about speaking out loud to them; they will be listening. Also, keep reminding yourself that you will be together again in the afterlife, after fulfilling your purpose in life. Then, if the two of you agree to it, go back to that moment in time in the space-time continuum and resume a life together at a moment and time before your soulmate's death. Even though this is a possibility, it is much more fun being together again in the afterlife than on Earth.

Can everyone who dies in a mass death be experiencing their purpose in life?

Yes. There may be a situation that exists on Earth that needs the attention of humankind worldwide and something needs to be done about it sooner than later. Given mass deaths have much greater impact on society than the death of one person, the death of a high number of people can be the purpose for all the soul/spirits to die.

Hitler's mass atrocities got to the point where humankind finally said: "*This is not right and it has to stop.*" The killing of many people over a period of years due to their belief system, race, or skin color are additional issues currently being addressed by society. The number of these killings has reached a point that the message sent is: "*Something is wrong, and something needs to be done.*"

Natural disasters occur for a reason and will continue to be accompanied by mass numbers of deaths. One message from disasters could be that better measures should be created to forecast these tragedies so nature can run its course without costing so many lives. The same is true from deaths in plane crashes or collapsing manmade structures. The message sent is technology must improve to prevent deaths from manmade objects and structures.

Why choose going back to Earth to avoid death rather than go to Heaven?

The primary reason people return to life on Earth and all it challenges is to fulfill their purpose in life. I believe it is very common for those who died unexpectedly (i.e. from accidents, natural disasters, murders) before they fulfilled their life's purpose to return to Earth.

Once they understand that Heaven will always be there, death is not feared but welcomed and looked forward to after fulfilling their life on Earth.

Why don't I remember experiencing Phase 3 after returning to my life?

Many people do remember. There are books and articles written about people and their experiences of life after death. Not all experiences are the same because each individual experiences the afterlife based on their belief system. Many people bring back messages from the afterlife to inform others or to fulfill their purpose in life. Others do not remember their return from death because it can interfere with experiencing something to fully understand what they are here to experience.

What will happen next after viewing the first two movies of my life?

I'll have one of two choices to make: either return to my life prior to my death or move on to Phase 4, which is Heaven. If I choose Heaven, I'll have to view the third movie I call: "What If?" This will be another rerun of my autobiography but with a little twist—I get to make as many different choices and decisions along the space-time continuum as I want and see what would have happened.

The Greatest Mysteries of Life and Beyond Life

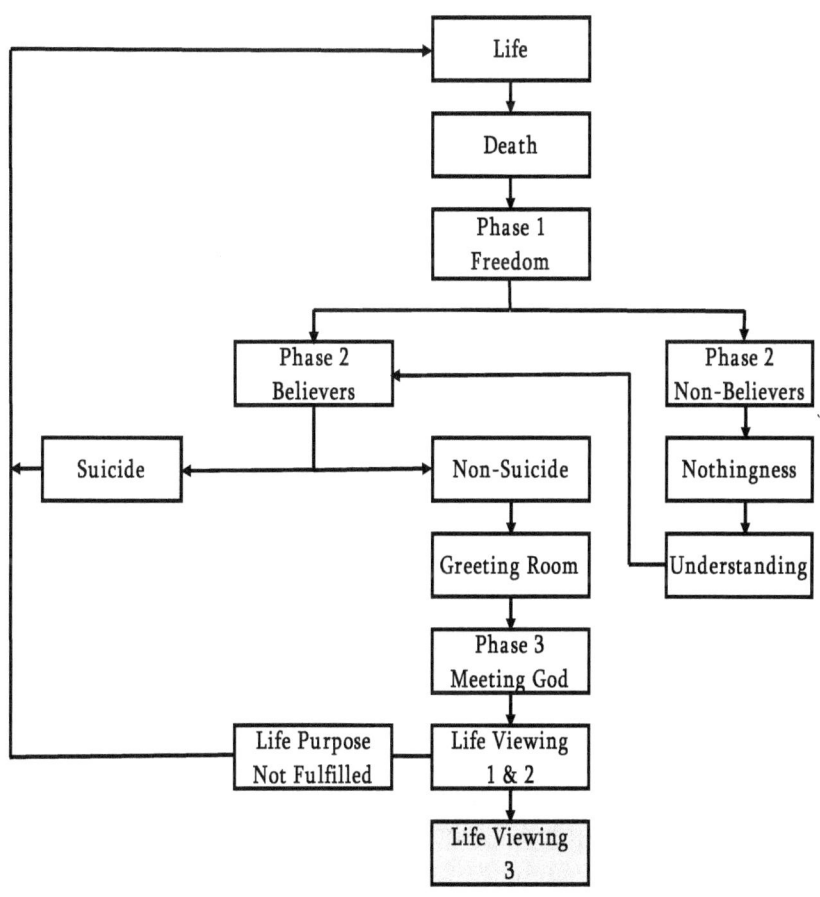

Along with the fun of God and me watching this movie, there are two reasons for this viewing: to satisfy my curiosity and for the lessons learned, through which we are able to move closer and closer to reaching the highest level of consciousness and total fulfillment.

Obviously, there can be an unlimited number of decisions and choices I might make along the way and an equal number of lessons learned. I think the following lessons will be among those learned by many spirit/souls.

Live one day at a time but co-create a plan for the future. Life is short and unpredictable and the only thing guaranteed is today. It is very important to live in the moment and appreciate each day, one at a time. To enjoy and live one day at a time, I have created a lifestyle plan and am using each day in the moment of now as stepping stones to the plan. It is my thoughts, words, and actions of today that create my future, so I have to be conscious of the value of each and every day and the importance of each and every thought, word, and action.

Lasting happiness is a state of mind. We can choose to be happy or we can choose to be unhappy in any circumstance. We can take short-term happiness into long-term happiness by controlling our state of mind from within and not letting external circumstances and resulting negative thoughts control our state of mind. We are responsible for creating our own happiness and we should not depend on other people or things for it. Long, lasting happiness is something we choose and create through our state of mind; it is not something that is pursued.

Make peace with our past. The negative by-products of not letting go of our past are stress, unhappiness, and regret. Each of these negative by-products can be harmful for a lifetime but the feel-good release of past issues occurs in a few minutes. Not letting go robs us of our happiness and doesn't allow us to live in the moment of now. By letting go, through forgiveness of our self or others, we are able to live a happier life, one day at a time.

Possessions are not as important than family and friend experiences. The pleasure and joy of positive experiences with our family, loved ones, and close friends far outweigh any material possessions we really did not need.

Choose a career of passion, not money. A career of passion, combined with a purpose, is far more rewarding than a career of less passion and a larger paycheck. If we happen to create a career of passion and are fortunate enough to be highly compensated, remember to use the money to create lasting memories, not to accumulate material possessions. A profession full of purpose and meaning creates a lifetime of fulfillment, if lived in a grateful and humble way.

Marry values and interests. There is no such thing as a perfect marriage and there is no magic bullet to guarantee a successful marriage. But we improve the odds when we can be our self and let our partner be themselves. Shared common interests are the fun things couple do together but there will be and should be different interests, which are acceptable as long as the one partner supports the other in their interest.

In my vision of the afterlife I will learn it won't really matter what path I took; they all will lead me to the same place in the end. I also believe I will come to accept myself for who I am. I already believe everything happens or does not happen for a reason. There are lessons to be learned from each experience that did or did not happen and without one experience, the next experience wouldn't have come along that could have a profound positive effect on our life. In the end, God and I will be at peace with who and what I was and also with the choices and decisions I did or did not make.

What happens when I reach Heaven?

Everyone creates their own Heaven. When we die, we will first experience exactly what our conscious (mind) believes it will look like. The setting will be exactly as we envisioned, along with the people who greeted us in Phase 2. If we believe we will be with Jesus, Buddha, or Muhammad and embraced by their unconditional love, then they will be there to lovingly greet and spend time with us. We'll be with any of our pets as well as with any other animal. In my Heaven, all animals are peaceful, so go hug a lion. There can also be any kind of place to call our Heavenly home—an island hut, mountaintop cabin, or mansion. We can go wherever we want, do whatever we want, see whoever we want, from Leonardo de Vinci to a favorite actor. The other ultra-cool aspect of the Heaven I envision is that we have access to the ultimate truthful answer to any question. Just ask the question and the answer will come at the speed of thought. After experiencing our self-created Heaven, we will experience the other part of Heaven: the real Heaven that is everything that is.

The Greatest Mysteries of Life and Beyond Life

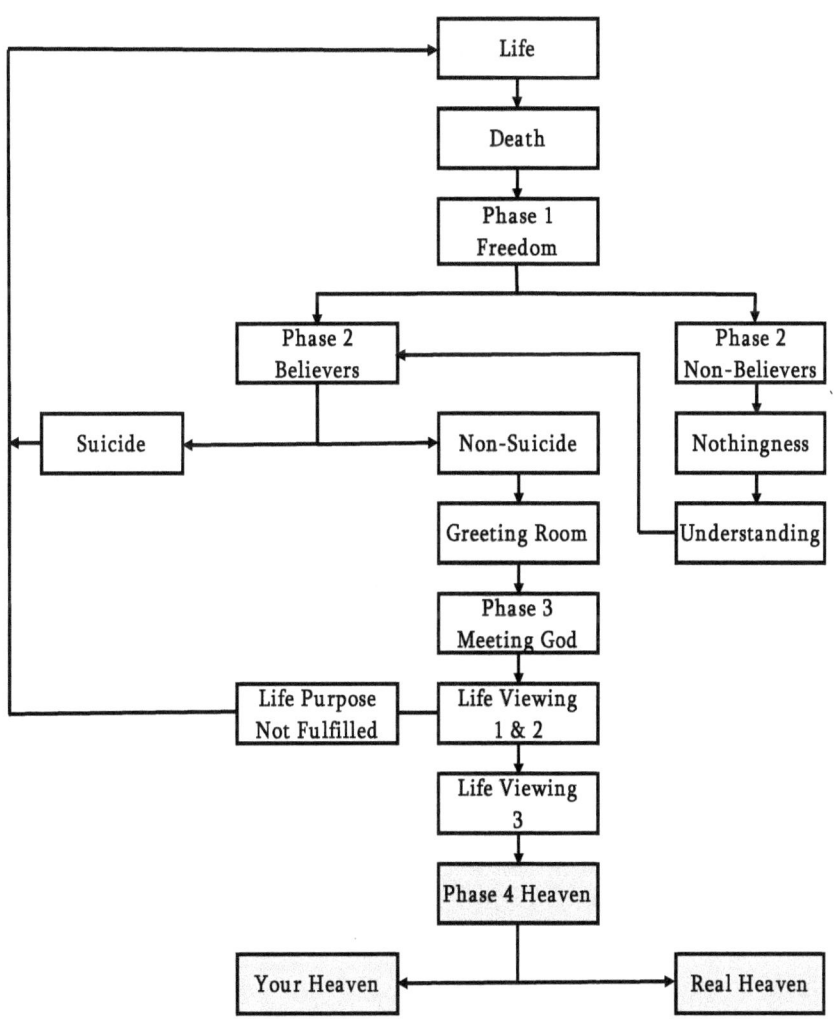

This other part of Heaven is the entire expanse of the Universe. Since we will again be a spirit of pure light, we will be part of and actually become the Universe with all of the other spirit light daughters and sons of God, sharing and floating in and around the Universe. The difference between the light we experience on Earth and the light in the Universe is that on Earth, we cannot see the rays of the light, only what they shine upon, whereas in the Universe, all the spirit lights can be seen and each spirit light has a different, indescribably beautiful color with rays of light that radiant love, compassion, wisdom, kindness, and acceptance.

While in the real Heaven, we'll be able to go anywhere in the Universe at any point in time at the speed of thought and, being a light means we can be in many different places at one time. Float among the stars, visit the countless number of planets and galaxies, meet the spirit lights of other planets, their way of life and what they looked like while taking on their physical form on their planet. Float to any time and place on Earth that was before our time or after and observe what took place and why. Visit the spirit lights of those relatives who passed on during our lifetime, see all our future relatives. The real Heaven also allows us access to the ultimate truthful answer to any question. Just ask the question and the answer will come.

There are no words to describe the feeling we'll experience in our Heaven and the real Heaven. The closest earthly description is an infinite feeling of love, total bliss unlike any other that can be ever imagined, and it really, really, really feels good!

Where is our Heaven?

The Heaven we created has its own special place within the realm of the space-time continuum.

Why did God create Heaven?
God created Heaven as a place to experience unconditional and unlimited love, peacefulness, and all that is good and beautiful.

Do animals go to Heaven?

Yes, all of God's animal creations go to Heaven. We will see our pets in Heaven as well as all other animals, large and small.

Are there angels in Heaven?

Yes, all the spirit daughters and sons created by God are angels. As mentioned before, upon creation of the space-time continuum, God created pieces of Itself and called these pieces spirits. All these spirits are angels.

What do angels do?

While the spirits/angels are in Heaven, they can do anything they want. They can also help those spirit/angels who are already incarnated as a soul by being a guardian angel or helper. Since we, as humans, are a triune of body, mind, and spirit and all spirits are angels, we humans are all one-third angel. During those times when our body, mind, and spirit work together and perform angelic acts of compassion, empathy, and other generous unconditional acts, we are call angels on Earth by others.

How long can I stay in Heaven?

We can stay in Heaven as long as we want, until the time comes when we want to go.

Why would anyone want to leave Heaven?

The spirit's mission is to evolve spiritually to a higher and higher level of consciousness and self-realization in order to strive toward total oneness with God. Since spirits are daughters and sons of God, they are already one with God but not at the highest level of consciousness as God.

There will come a time, while in Heaven, when the spirit is ready to continue experiencing more and more in order to evolve toward oneness with God. In Heaven, everything can be understood conceptually but cannot be fully felt and truly understood unless felt experientially. When this time comes, the spirit is ready for Phase 5: communion.

I believe we may become bored in Heaven after we have seen, done, and talked to everyone we wanted to. The things we can do are endless and it will depend upon our imagination. There is ultimate knowledge of why things happen and places to see throughout the universe, but I believe a spirit can only understand them conceptually. There will come a time when we are ready to leave Heaven and continue on as the creative spirit we are.

What happens during Phase 5: communion?

During communion, our spirit light becomes immersed within and in communion with the spirit of God as one. At this time, our spirit light and God will first decide on the experience(s) they wish to attempt to create and thus experience while incarnated as a soul of the human in the next lifetime.

The Greatest Mysteries of Life and Beyond Life

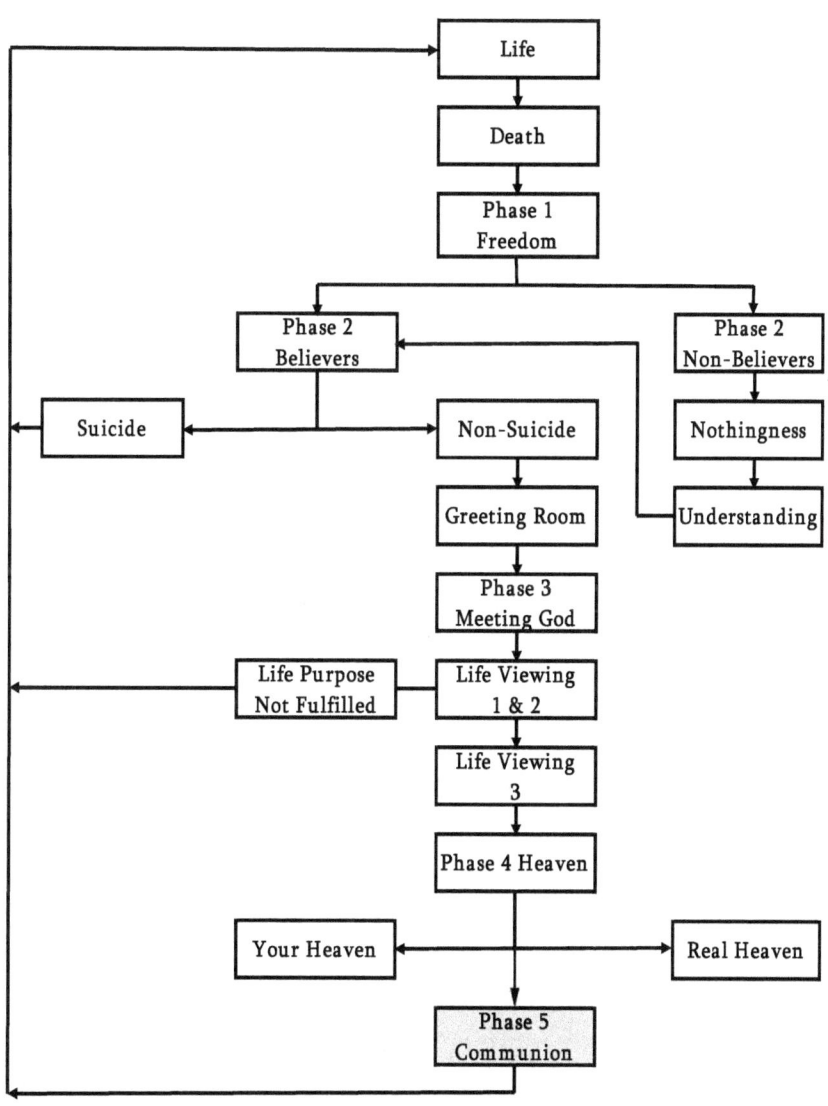

Next comes the planning process, which includes who will be the mother, the father, and what place and time to be born to begin the creative process. Once completed, the cycle of life is completed once again, as the spirit light is reincarnated as a soul in the womb of the mother.

How does the spirit know what it wants to experience or do prior to reincarnation?

The three life viewings during meeting with God—especially the "What If" movies—have a major impact on what the spirit wants to experience or do in the next lifetime. I envision that, during the viewings, there will be times when I'll have a wow moment—maybe of another lifestyle or profession, or to be homeless or to wander the world—and wonder what it would be like. Maybe I'll want to explore what life would be like on another planet in another galaxy.

The list of what I want to experience may be long or it may be only one thing, like being a messenger or teacher to bring attention to the world the issues that need to be addressed or overcome to help humanity move forward and constructively from a local and worldwide perspective.

Each spirit's mission of what to do and experience is unique and individual from one soul to another. The reason for the soul to experience something is that it allows the spirit to grow incrementally toward a higher level of consciousness and total oneness with God. God's desire for all spirits is to arrive at the highest level of consciousness and thus total fulfillment. At the highest level of consciousness and total fulfillment, the spirit totally understands everlasting love, peace, joy, acceptance, gratefulness, and blessedness. Total fulfillment is God's wish for all Its daughter and son offspring.

What can be learned by understanding the five phases of death?

- There is a God.

- God is unconditional love.

- God is the great creator of all that is seen and unseen and the co-creator with Its spirit daughters and sons.

- God does not need or want anything. God desires what our spirit desires.

- God is grace.

- We never really die. Our spirit lives forever; only our body and mind die.

- We are creative spirits. We create everything as a soul/spirit during our life on Earth due to our freedom of choice. When we die, we create our own Heaven. We chose to create our experience in the real Heaven. We chose to create who and what we want to be from one lifetime to the next.

- Hell does not physically exist but can only exist in the afterlife if our belief system believes so. We are the creator of our afterlife. If we believe we will or may go to Hell after death then we will be in our self-created Hell. Fortunately, the belief of a Hell in the afterlife will dissolve during Phase 2 of death.

What is God's grace?

There are many different definitions of God's grace. Many will say it cannot be defined but only felt and we know it when it happens. I define it as God's unmerited favor and willingness to give to Its daughters and sons the free will of choice to be, do, or experience what they want to be from one lifetime to the next.

Why do some people appear to have more of God's grace than another?

God is not the one who decides what one person is going to be, do, or experience while on Earth. It is each of us communing with God prior to being incarnated as a soul at conception that decides who and what we want to be. It is by God's grace of freedom of choice that allows us the ability to accomplish or achieve what it is we want to be, do, or experience.

Why would anyone want to be born with a lifelong handicap or disease?

All of us come to Earth to be, do, or experience something, to be a messenger and/or teacher, or a combination of both. Someone may have decided to be handicapped or to have a disease at birth to be the one who helps find a cure. Without someone being handicapped or with a disease, a cure cannot be found. Someone with a handicap or disease also helps others meet their reason for being on Earth, to be a nurse, doctor, caregiver, technician, engineer, researcher, or whatever.

Also, someone who has a lifelong handicap or disease can be an inspiration to others and be a major contributor to society. I watched a documentary on a man born without any legs who competed as a wrestler. Helen Keller was blind and deaf and look at all she accomplished. Stephen Hawkins with ALS has contributed immensely to the world of science. Author, painter, and poet Christy Brown had cerebral palsy and could only move his left foot, yet communicated and was an inspiration. The list goes on and on.

If we choose, why would anyone want to be homeless, living under a bridge?

A spirit may have decided to be a homeless person in order to be a messenger. Let's say a homeless person collected enough money to eat a meager breakfast at a Denny's® restaurant. Sitting at a booth in front of the homeless person, with their backs to him, was a mother and daughter. The child turned around and looked at the homeless man. The mother turned around, saw the homeless man and was shocked at his ragged appearance, telling her daughter not to look at him. The daughter turned around again and, with a big smile on his face, the homeless man put his thumbs in his ears and waved to her with his fingers. Both the child and the man laughed, but the mother quickly grabbed her daughter and told her to sit straight and stop looking at the man. The girl jumped up and turned around again and the man was opening and closing his hands in front of his face playing peek-a-boo. Both the homeless man and child laughed again, drawing the attention of others in the restaurant. The mother grabbed her daughter and told her to sit straight ahead immediately.

The mother and daughter, as well as the homeless man, got up to pay for their respective meal, with the homeless man standing behind the mother and daughter in line. The mother was holding her daughter in her arms and the daughter was looking back at the homeless man. The daughter reached out her arms in an effort to give the homeless man a hug. The mother initially resisted but, at the persistence of her daughter, she relented. The girl wrapped her little arms around the man's neck, laid her head on his shoulder and the homeless man patted her softly on her back. There were tears running down the homeless man's cheek, the mother's cheek, and others in the restaurant. The message sent to the mother and others at the restaurant was that the little girl showed unconditional love toward the homeless man, which is something we all need to practice. Even if this one event and the message it sent to the mother and the others in the restaurant was the sole purpose of the homeless man's life, wasn't it worth it?

Another message sent by those who are disadvantaged in some way is not to compare our grace to the grace of another. Do not compare our decision on who we want to be, do, or experience in life to what someone else chooses to be, do, or experience. Do not judge another person's grace, for we cannot truly understand and experience their grace. We may try to put ourselves in their state of grace but we can never experience their true grace; we can only truly experience and understand our own grace.

Religions

Are religions bad?

Religions are neither good nor bad; they exist for a purpose. Positive aspects of religion include increased hope and optimism by providing answers to the unanswerable and incomprehensible questions, which in turn fosters a healthy positive attitude. Religions also promote a feeling of belonging; it's been said a key ingredient to a happy life is a sense of belonging, which in turn promotes physiological, mental, and physical health.

Why do religions exist?

Religions are man-made and exist to help people make sense of existential questions and incomprehensible events they encounter in life. Religions also exist as a source of strength during challenging times and a source of compassion and love in times of pain or loss.

Belief systems based on religion are handed down from one generation to the next, with each new generation told not to challenge their belief and to view all other beliefs as wrong. For the most part, people don't explore other religions, because humans are essentially followers and will continue to do so as long as their religion meets their expectations, has structure, and is clear and rigid. Individuals have a hesitancy to challenge their belief systems or explore for their own truths out of fear, so religions continue from generation to generation.

Why are there different religions?

Religions exist as an attempt to make sense of the unanswerable and incomprehensible questions about life and events. This essentially creates a blank slate for any group of people to create answers to the unanswerable and incomprehensible questions about life and events and create a religion around them.

What is the right religion?

Given there is no possible way to prove beyond a shadow of doubt the answers to the unanswerable questions, no religion can claim their religion is the absolutely right religion. The only right religion is the belief system built around each individual's view of the unanswerable and incomprehensive questions. This does not mean that other religions or people cannot help lead us to our truth, but our answers to the unanswerable and incomprehensive questions must come from our internal voice. Don't be swayed by what is said in this book or from any other person or religious institution that professes to be the source of the answers. Just listen and let the internal voice be our source to the answers to the unanswerable and incomprehensive questions. Respect everyone's opinion and each institution's truths, but rely on our internal voice for our truth. In the end, I don't believe it matters what our beliefs are, what religion we follow or if we're agnostic or atheist. We all end up in the same place when we die.

Our truth resides deep within our soul. The purity of our truth cannot come from another belief system or person, only from within by going to our place of peace and feeling it.

Our truth cannot come from our mind or intellect, which only gives us a projection of what we believe and not what we truly feel. The projection of a beautiful sunset described by another or seen in a photograph won't have the same impact as being there and feeling the warmth, beauty, serenity, and truth of a sunset. The feelings of our heart and soul express our truth.

Is it acceptable to be an atheist or agnostic?

Yes, it is. Atheism is a belief system that connects people who do not believe there is a God. Agnosticism is a belief system that connects people who don't know if there is a God. Based on the definition of religion—a particular belief system that connects people—atheism, and agnosticism are both religions.

It is important to understand that atheism, agnosticism, and other non-theist religions play a very important role in helping those who believe in theist religions better understand their beliefs. Theist belief systems would not exist if non-theist beliefs did not exist and vice versa. I believe God created everything seen and unseen and thus relativity, so it follows that God created those who do not believe in God so those who do believe in God can better understand God and vice versa.

WAR

Is there ever a good reason for a country to start a war?

There are reasons for countries to start a war but never a good reason for one country to start a war against another country.

What are the reasons for a country to get involved in a war?

The main reason is to protect itself from an invading country. Another reason is to defend an allied country. Diplomacy should always be attempted first before going to war, which should be the last resort.

Why do countries start wars against other countries?

A country goes to war against another country out of greed for more land, for gaining access to mineral resources, superiority over a weaker or lesser country, hatred toward another country and their way of life, eliminating a group or sect of people, and differences in religious faith.

What are ways to prevent wars from starting?

The long-term approach is to address belief systems, cultural conditioning, social cultural conditioning, and integrity development. The short-term method is to discourage a country from wanting to go to war by creating a situation or condition where the loss will inevitable be greater than the gain, or where it's not possible to win.

How can these situations and conditions be stopped to prevent wars?

The answer is to utilize the existing global organizations, who have been inept in preventing war, massive crimes against humanity, and conflicts. There needs to be some reorganizing and modifications to these existing global peace-keeping organizations.

What global organizations need to be modified?

The United Nations, NATO, and many other regional organizations around the world have been established to help prevent wars from starting. But the world is still in a fragile and volatile position, for another major worldwide conflict could break out at any time. It is apparent, with more and more countries having nuclear, chemical, and biological weapons available, the next World War will truly be the war of unimaginable destruction and loss of life. As Einstein once stated: *"I know not with what weapons World War III will be fought but World War IV will be fought with sticks and stones."*

The problem with these global peacekeeping bodies or organizations is there is a body to carry out the intellectual decision of the organization's mind but with no input from the organization's soul and/or spirit. From this analogy, what needs to be included with the leaders and politicians of these organizations are highly-recognized spiritual leaders to represent humankind and bring the spiritual aspect to the decision-making process; not a religious element, but a spiritual element.

This spiritual group needs to be included as an equal voice in these peacekeeping organizations to bring the human element into the picture. The qualities brought by the spiritual element are that greed is not good; there are enough resources, food, water, love, and kindness to go around; no one person, race, culture or creed is superior than another; hatred does not exist between any race, culture, or nationality; killing for the purpose of gain or in the name of God is prohibited.

What is the long-term solution to prevent social upheaval?

War seems to be a constant in our lives. Conflicts are a global occurrence. Social issues and challenges continue and are getting worse. From a global point of view, these issues will continue to grow and we will continue moving backward as long as the rate at which we create new and improved ways to kill one other keeps moving faster than attempts to find ways to get along. We need to change our belief system.

Wars and conflicts occur because people act based on what they believe is right. There is no such thing as bad people, only bad decisions, made by inherently good people, based on what they believe. Some people are taught to believe that certain races and classes of people are superior, leaving others to feel underestimated, marginalized, and undervalued, which causes social upheaval. Some believe their religion is the only religion and kill those of other faiths. A country may feel their way of life is threatened by limited resources or another country's way of life and believe the only way to solve the problem is to go to war against them.

If enough people make the same bad decision based on what they believe, it can lead to social upheaval, major conflicts, and war. So, we need to change what people are taught to believe. We are influenced and culturally conditioned by our belief systems and by social conditions. The cultural conditioning by our belief system and social condition is what I define as our influence arenas. A long-term solution in preventing wars and to move society forward is to modify our influence arenas.

Another area that has an impact on what we believe, and thus how we react and make decisions, is one's personal level of integrity, which means having strong life values.

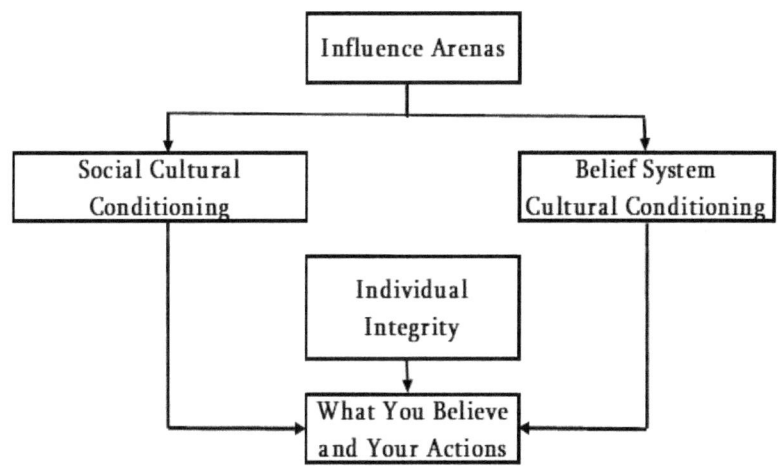

CULTURAL CONDITIONING

What is "belief system cultural conditioning?"

Belief system cultural conditioning is the process of passing down, from one generation to the next, belief systems values, practices, and beliefs. These belief systems are not only the traditional religions of the world, but also agnosticism, atheism, and other non-religious traditions. The members of each belief system are conditioned to believe their belief is the one truth and other belief systems are wrong. A vast majority of a belief system's values, practices, and beliefs are passed down to the children, primarily by their parents, their place of worship, and those belief systems within an educational system that is part of the place of worship. Therefore, if a belief system passes on beliefs that cause fear, anxiety, and conflict, these conditions will continue from one generation to the next.

What is social cultural conditioning?

Social culture conditioning is the process of passing down, from one generation to the next of a particular large group of people, similar and unique characteristics, patterns of behavior, experiences, and knowledge as defined by their birthplace, appearance, language, cuisine, social habits, lifestyle, communication, music, and arts. The groups of people within each culture consider their culture to be the norm and it weighs heavily onto their thought and decision-making processes, how others are treated, their manner of speaking, what is consider right and wrong, how to dress, etc. Those responsible for the evolution of social cultural conditioning are authority figures, such as parents, the educational system, the political systems, religions, peers, and both social and visual mediums.

Even though all cultures do have many positive aspects, it is those few negative labels that cause fear, anxiety, conflicts, and wars.

INTEGRITY

What is individual integrity?

Individual integrity is being consistently honest, true to oneself, and having a strong set of positive life values.

What is the definition of a person of high integrity?

A person of high integrity makes sound and upright decisions, based on their internal voice, spoken from the heart, not the mind. When friends and family are on our side, we do the right thing. When family and friends are not on our side, we do the right thing. When something is easy to do, we do the right thing. When something is hard to do, we do the right thing. When there are low chances of negative consequences of our decision, we do the right thing. When there are high chances of negative consequences of our decision, we do the right thing. When we are afraid to make a decision, we make the right decision. When we are not afraid to make a decision, we do the right thing. When others are watching, we do the right thing. When others are not watching, we do the right thing.

How do we know when the choice is from the heart or mind?

If the choice is from the mind, it may not have high integrity, because it's subject to thought and rationalization. The mind has the ability to make a self-choice and not necessarily the right choice. When making a choice from the mind there is also the possibility of someone talking us out of it. Also, choices from the mind sometimes are the most convenient choice and not the right choice.

There is a litmus test to help decide if our choice is from the heart or mind: Do we want other people to know what we've decided. Suppose we see someone drop their wallet. We pick it up with the intention of giving it back and then discover $300 inside. Our mind immediately says: "*Keep the wallet; we can use the money. Anyone who carries that much around can afford to lose the money.*" Then our heart says: "*Giving it back is the right thing to do; it's his money, he earned it, and has a purpose for the money.*" Now the litmus test: what would we do if we knew whatever we decided would be broadcast on the news and Internet for all to know?

Why is it important to live a life of high integrity?

Integrity informs every aspect of our life, from work to relationships. There are many reasons why living a life of integrity is important, it:

- Creates an authentic person with a high level of self-confidence in everything said and done, creating peace of mind at not having to question or look over our shoulder.

- Develops an aura of trust, honesty, and leadership with our family, friends, co-workers, and others observing our actions and what we say

MODIFICATIONS TO CULTURAL CONDITIONING

Why are modifications to social cultural conditions necessary?

An individual's decisions and beliefs are made based partly on cultural conditioning. Unfortunately, one culture's views and beliefs are often in direct conflict with another culture's views and beliefs. This can result in conflicts, mistrust, and wars. To prevent the possibility of wars, conflicts, and social upheaval, cultures need modifying.

The business world is constantly changing and adapting to grow and move forward. Technology continues evolving to make life better for all. Medicine is constantly researching and advancing to provide better physical care for all. I think we also need to address upgrading belief systems to help make life better for all from a spiritual point of view.

What guideline should be used to determine what modifications are made?

One guideline businesses use when making modifications is to make all decisions in alignment with their mission statement. In general, a mission statement describes what a company stands for and their values. I consider this to be a universal cultural conditioning mission statement: "*To create a social culture that will promote world peace and harmony.*"

I think most cultures would agree with this mission statement.

What cultural modifications need to be made to promote world peace and harmony?

Before identifying those topics, I think cultures need to upgrade and/or modify. I want to be clear that I am not suggesting eliminating any existing culture. Every culture has historical paths, traits, unique and timeless characteristics, positive aspects, a sense of belongingness, and an identity that can only remain if each culture remains intact. I'm suggesting taking a closer look at all cultures and make changes designed to help reduce, as much as possible, any fears, anxieties, and misunderstandings with other cultures that can lead to hatred, anger, conflicts, and, in extreme cases, war. The current interaction between many cultures is creating a world none of us likes, but if we address what it is that creates fear, anxiety, and conflicts, there will be hope.

The major problem between cultures is the variety of negative viewpoints and actions that have been passed down from generation to generation, such as one culture is superior to another, so it is justified to undervalue, marginalize, harm, and even kill because of cultural differences. To align with the social cultural conditioning mission statement, I believe the following modifications need to be taught by all cultures:

No culture, race, or person is superior or inferior to another.

- We all have different talents and skills, but that does not mean one person or culture is better than another. We are all gifted in one way or another but the gift does not make one superior to another. One may be the

- president of the United States and another may be a janitor, but it does not make one superior to the other; they just have different levels of responsibilities.
- Every human being has a purpose on Earth and, thus, everyone is special, no matter their race, culture, or actions experienced during their lifetime.

No one race, or culture is to be undervalued, underestimated, or marginalized.

- God created all the different races and cultures for the variety and pleasure of their many differences. When human beings create something, we also create variety; that's why we have different cars, airplanes, fashion, hairstyles, etc. Even if we do not have an appreciation for what a race or culture brings to the world, appreciate the variety in life.

Harming anyone because of cultural differences is never acceptable.

- The classic example of this is the racial tension between the white police culture and African American culture currently afflicting the US. White police are causing pain and, in extreme circumstances, killing African American people due to their culture. In retaliation, African Americans are killing white policemen. This behavior will continue until a belief is in place that killing another based-on culture is wrong and unacceptable.

- History has seen cultural clashes for millennia. A very small sampling of atrocities between cultures include those against those of Jewish descent, the Native Americans, people of different sexual orientation, poor people against rich people—the list goes on and on.

- It is imperative to have an open mind to potentially controversial modifications. It is also important for the leaders of belief systems, including atheists and agnostics, to come together and have an open, non-confrontational, and candid dialogue about these items as well as where our society is heading from a humanistic point of view.

The following are the major modifications I believe each religion and belief system needs to discuss and agree upon.

There is no one religion that is the right religion

- There are too many belief systems and non-theist beliefs today that profess their system is the only one. Given there is no positive proof to any answers given for unanswerable questions, no belief system can say theirs is the absolute truth. Respect all belief systems and do not ridicule, mock, or judge those of other belief systems.

Do not kill others in the name of religion

- There are certain religions that permit killing non-believers. Of all the upgrades with the various religions and belief systems that need to be addressed, this one is at the top of the list. It is hard to fathom how many killings, major conflicts, and wars were fought throughout history, resulting in millions of lives lost, based on the various belief systems and religions.

The essence of who we are individually never dies

- The essence of who we are is a spirit, and when our body and mind die, our spirit remains. There are too many people who don't understand death and live fearing of death, which can lead to anxiety and depression.

There is no such physical place as Hell

- Teach that Hell does not physically exist but can only exist in the afterlife if our belief system believes so. We are the creator of our afterlife. If we believe we will or may go to Hell after death then we will be in our self-created Hell. Fortunately, the belief of a Hell in the afterlife will dissolve during Phase 2 of death. After the realization of Hell is non-existent, teach that one's spirit will move on and live forever.

God is a loving God and not one to be feared

- God is a loving God of total compassion, unconditional love, and forgiveness. God should not be feared, because there is nothing we can say, be, or do that will stop God from loving us, whether we believe there is a God or not.

God listens and talks to everyone, whether we are a believer or not

- Two of the greatest gifts humans possess are the free will of choice and the ability to be divinely inspired through communication with God. God does not physically talk to us but speaks in other ways. Some hear it through a quiet voice in their mind and heart. Others hear it in dreams, some through the voice of family and loved ones, or through thoughts when awakened in the middle of the night. We all can have a dialogue with God; find our way. If one's belief system does not believe in the divine, teach that everyone has the ability to be inspired and to listen to the voice in our mind and heart.

Even if the leaders of the various belief and non-belief systems agree upon the modifications, it will take a several generations for the positive effects of these upgrades to take full effect. That is why addressing these issues is a long-term strategy. Over time, these upgrades will be second nature and a start toward reducing fears, anxieties, and conflicts.

The good news is the process appears to have begun. Pope Francis is the leader of one of the largest religious institutions of world and he has recently said the following:

"We cannot insult the faith of others. We cannot make fun of the faith of others. There is a limit. Every religion has its dignity."

"Hatred is not to be carried in the name of God and war is not to be waged in the name of God."

"Let no one use God as a shield while planning and carrying out acts of violence and oppression."

"May no one use religion as a pretext for actions against the fundamental rights of every man and woman."

"He (God) created human beings and let them develop according to the internal laws that he gave to each one so they would reach their fulfillment."

Similar to what Pope Francis has begun, all leaders of all belief systems should begin a path toward upgrading their religion.

Why is it important for one to have a belief system?

During our lifetime, we will be faced with many experiences and events that cause us to ask existential questions. Forming a belief system allows us to come up with answers that can't be proven right or wrong, but are based upon our individual belief system, which allows us to move on with life and become who and what we want to be.

Another reason for forging a belief system is that we are informed by what we believe and our decisions are based on what we believe.

BUILDING INTEGRITY

How can we instill integrity to reduce war, conflicts, and social upheaval?

Each one of us needs to look in the mirror and ask: "*What level of integrity am I conveying to others by what I say, what I do, and where I go?*" If we honestly feel we are lacking, make a promise to strive toward being a person of high integrity.

Next, all children need to be taught at an early age a set of life values and positive self-thoughts to begin building their emotional intelligence about themselves. Parents and guardians need to teach children life values, positive self-thoughts, and emotional intelligence prior to them starting elementary school. Once in school, life values, positive self-thoughts, and emotional intelligence will be reinforced by having lessons teaching integrity built into their curriculum.

The following are the life values, positive self-thoughts, and emotional intelligence to include in the lesson or curriculum.

Public Elementary/Middle School
Self-Thoughts
- Be happy who we re
- Do not put down ourselves.
- We are special and one of a kind.

Life Values
- Obey our mother and father.
- Do not willfully kill an animal or plant for no reason.
- Do not steal.

- Do not lie.

Public High School
Self-Thoughts
- Love ourselves unconditionally and be happy who we are.
- Do not put down ourselves.
- Everyone, no matter how they look or their culture, has a purpose in life.
- Teach what integrity is and the importance of having a high integrity.

Life Values
- Do the right thing, always.
- Honor our mother and father.
- Make quiet time to think or meditate.
- Do not willfully kill another person, animal or plant for no reason or without cause or justification.
- Do not steal.
- Do not lie.
- Do not commit adultery.

Emotional Intelligence
- Understand emotional intelligence.

Parochial Elementary/Middle School
Self-Thoughts
- Be happy who we are. God created us just the way we are.

- Do not put down ourselves. God loves us just the way we are.
- We are special and one of a kind because we are a child of God.

Life Values

- Obey our mother and father.
- Do not willfully kill an animal or plant for no reason.
- Do not steal.
- Do not lie.

Parochial High School

Self-Thoughts

- Love ourselves unconditionally, and be happy who we are.
- God created us just the way we are.
- Do not put ourselves-down.
- God has a reason for our life.
- No matter how they look, their culture, or belief, everyone has a purpose in life.
- Teach what integrity is and the importance of having a high integrity.

Life Values

- Do the right thing, always.
- Honor our mother and father.
- Make time to be with ourselves and be with God.
- Make quiet time pray prayers of gratitude and gratefulness.

- Do not willfully kill another person, animal, or plant without cause or justification.
- Do not steal.
- Do not lie.
- Do not commit adultery.
- There is no one religion that is the right religion.
- Study others' belief systems.
- There is no such physical place as Hell.
- Teach that God talks to and with all who will listen.
- Teach about social cultural conditioning.
- Teach about death and what happens when we die

Emotional Intelligence

- Understand emotional intelligence.

The next challenge is to initiate a movement to incorporate these self-thoughts and values in all public, private, religious, and home-taught curriculums worldwide, from elementary and middle school to high school. Nothing is more important than the future of our children and the state of humanity worldwide.

How can I be a messenger of social and belief system cultural conditioning changes?

Most people do not see themselves as messengers. Humankind has been waiting and searching for "the one" messenger to come along for millennia. Some messengers of the past include Buddha, Muhammed, Jesus, the Dali Lamas, Gandhi, Confucius, etc. Each of them created a movement that made a difference and a positive change.

We need to believe each and every one of us is a messenger. The only way we cannot be a messenger is if we did not exist. Every thought we have, word we speak, and action we take is a message. Each of these messages are observed by others—our family, those close to us, co-workers, even strangers—so our message can have as big an impact as the messengers listed above because the messages others receive will then pass on to people they know by their thoughts, words, and action. Eventually, the message can help all of humankind by upgrading our belief system, addressing our social conditioning issues, reducing fears and anxieties, and stopping useless loss of life with wars and conflicts.

How can I have the greatest impact as a messenger?

If I want to have impact, I need to start with the social cultural conditioning of my immediate family members. Next, I must make an effort with the public, private, and religious educational systems to make these social cultural conditioning issues a part of their curriculum. I need to emphasize that, with each family member and school curriculum, no culture, race, or person is superior to or inferior to another; no one race or culture is to be undervalued, underestimated, or marginalized; and killing of another due to cultural differences is never acceptable.

Another step I can take is to meet with the leaders of my belief system and bring my message to them directly about making these changes or at least bring them to the attention of the congregation.

Another method of creating an impact on making change is to move away from the "single messenger" concept to a group movement.

How do I start a movement?

Movements happen by mobilizing the collective energy of people united by a shared purpose. There is no one step-by-step methodology for starting and sustaining a movement. There's no magic formula and the steps used in one successful movement may not be successful in another movement. That said, I think there are some common factors to most successful movements. The movement must be something people can associate with and can believe in. It needs a leader—or leaders—with the passion, unwavering drive, and belief in the issue who is not afraid to stand up and say what needs to be said, no matter the consequences. Leaders attract others they feel can share the same conviction and belief.

The initial followers must be energized, compelled, and inspired by the leader's vision. There is no longer a lone leader but a small group of people with the same vision. It is important the leader welcomes followers as equals and that the movement is about the issue and not the leader. This opens up the opportunity for many others to follow. The next set of followers become the Pied Pipers of the movement; these people are the ones that get the word out, are well-connected, know how to use social media, and make others feel safe jumping into the movement.

EMOTIONS AND EMOTIONAL INTELLIGENCE

What is emotional intelligence?

My definition of emotional intelligence is the ability to be aware of, express, control, and manage the feelings felt when reacting to an emotion.

What are emotions and feelings?

An emotion is a natural, uncontrollable, measurable, instantaneous neurological and chemical process in the brain in response to an external or internal stimulus. Feelings are the unmeasurable associations and conscious reactions to an emotion. Feelings describe the sensation felt after the release of the chemicals to the brain and body by the brain. They help us make meaning of an emotion. Emotions are event-driven and a powerful by-product of the mind, whereas feelings are the by-product of our belief system.

There are countless feelings one can experience, with the most common feelings being envy, anger, grief, fear, and love. The two primary and most important feelings are love and fear, because every thought, word, and action are based on either fear or love.

Why is it important to know and build one's emotional intelligence?

It is very important for each one of us to reach a healthy level of emotional intelligence in order to handle relationships, life issues, and challenges judiciously and empathetically. Being emotionally intelligent as an adult does not mean we won't experience emotions and feelings; it means we will be able to recognize emotions and feelings and be able to express, control, and manage them in a healthy way.

As an example, grief helps us face and deal with a loss; if we do not recognize and handle grief in a healthy way, we can become depressed and lose control of our life. Anger is a strong feeling of annoyance, displeasure, or hostility, often incited by a perceived wrong. When anger is not controlled and managed as an adult, it can result in unhealthy rage. Envy is resentment, discontent, or covetousness with regard to someone else's advantages, success, recognition, possessions, etc. and the desire to have the same. Envy can be a healthy emotion if used to understand our deepest desires or aspirations and if it is used a motivator. We have control when experiencing and managing envy, but when we have no control we experience jealousy, hatred, low self-esteem, and aggressiveness. Fear is a survival mechanism to protect us and help the body survive. Some fears are inherent, such as fear of darkness or of fire. We have control when experiencing and managing fear, but when we have no control, we go into panic mode.

If each one of us can individually reach a healthy level of emotional intelligence, we will be better equipped to face the challenges and issues of everyday life. By individually achieving a healthy level of emotional intelligence, we can collectively begin to feel we are all one as a worldwide race, which will begin the process of healing the Earth, preventing social and cultural upheaval, and senseless conflicts and wars. That's why it's important our children, at an early age, learn to express and understand their emotions in a healthy manner.

WE ARE ALL ONE

How will understanding we are all one improve world condition?

I believe, if we all truly understand and believe without hesitation that we are all one as a human race, over time, conflicts and wars between races and different cultures will be greatly reduced and eventually end. It does not mean disagreements and arguments cease, but conflicts and problems will be handled differently. Going to war, killing massive numbers of people and destruction of property will become a thing of the past.

If we believe, in our hearts we are all one as brothers and sisters worldwide, wars and major conflicts would eventually end and how we treat each other on a day-to-day basis would be a base to begin creating a Heaven on Earth scenario.

What is meant by "we are all one," and how can we all be one?

"We are all one" means that, from a humankind point of view, we are one great big worldwide family. Even though we may have different skin color and bone structure, it has been scientifically proven we are all comprised of the same molecular elements. Anatomically, we all are mammals with two legs, two arms, a torso, neck, head, and, within the body, we all have a brain and other internal organs.

We are also all one spiritually. When we are a spirit in our formless natural state, the essence of who we are is a light energy source. When the spirit becomes a soul after being incarnated with the human, it is absorbed into the body and mind, which creates a vibrating energy field in and around the body. This vibrating light energy source projects outward in all directions from the body, out into the universe and does not stop or ever end but becomes less and less radiant as it expands into the vastness of the universe, similar to how, when we point a flashlight up in the sky and turn it on, the light continues on and on but becomes less and less radiant. The planets we see in the sky are not actually the planets but a light energy source from each planet that has traveled many light years to our planet and continues to move past our planet, further into the universe.

With all the souls on Earth projecting their light energy field in all directions into the universe, these light energy fields will eventually become intertwined with each other, which is how we all become one, from a spiritual perspective.

This also explains why so many scientists, philosophers, religious leaders, gurus, shamans, etc., say we are all one with the universe. Not only are all the humans on Earth projecting their energy out into the universe, but all other living and non-living things on Earth are doing so as well, resulting in everything in the entire space-time continuum of the universe being as one.

What is preventing humanity from feeling we are all one?

We are not facing, addressing, and changing our viewpoint on the major issues with social cultural conditioning, not upgrading our belief system cultural conditioning, not maintaining a high level of integrity, and not understanding our spirits have different missions.

How is social cultural conditioning preventing movement toward oneness?

The primary reason social cultural conditioning is preventing the movement toward oneness is the divisiveness that has been created between the various races and cultures around the world.

How is belief system cultural conditioning preventing movement toward oneness?

The primary reason belief system cultural conditioning is preventing the movement toward oneness is that many belief systems cause anger and hatred toward other belief systems, creating social upheaval, major conflicts, and, in extreme cases, war.

How is one's level of integrity preventing movement toward oneness?

In order to address and accept those issues preventing movement toward oneness from a social and belief system cultural conditioning point of view, one needs to have a high level of integrity.

How is the spirit's mission on Earth preventing movement toward oneness?

The spirit's mission on Earth is not really preventing the movement toward oneness but part of the evolution toward oneness. As mentioned earlier, God gave spirits the ability to incarnate as souls with human beings, allowing God and the soul to experience the unlimited emotions and feelings of life, in order to move to a higher level of understanding, conscientious, and oneness with God. In order to truly understand an emotion or feeling, the opposite must exist and be experienced. So, I believe there are spirits incarnated in bodies to create fear, promote war, and cause separation in order to understand love, peace and what it feels like to be as one with humanity.

So, the separation of humanity will always exist so we can understand oneness?

No. When all spirits from their past lives have either caused war, been violent, created major conflicts, or been part of the separation from humanity, or been so closely related to these acts to the point that they are felt and understood, there will no longer be a need to experience war, violence, conflicts, and separation of humanity but love, peace, and oneness.

With so many different cultures, how can we become one?

We can begin by upgrading our current religions, addressing the social conditioning issues we face today, and strive to maintain a high level of individual integrity.

PRAYER

What is prayer?

I believe there are two types of prayers: one of co-creation and one of thanksgiving. A co-creation prayer is between an individual and God through the process of everything we think, say, and do. A prayer of thanksgiving is one to God in thanks for already taking care of some issue or outcome.

How does a co-creation prayer work?

Co-creation prayers occur every day throughout our life on Earth. Anything we think, say, or do is a co-creation prayer. Our part in the co-creation process with God is to listen to that small, quiet inner voice, feel and do the right thing, make the right and timely decisions, and always be aware of the creative steps sent by God to facilitate the prayer being answered. What is interesting about the co-creation prayer is it really is not a religious act, as most people associate a prayer to be, but an everyday act by all people, no matter what their religious belief is, or if they are an agnostic, or atheist.

What is a prayer of thanksgiving?

A prayer of thanksgiving is really the only prayer we all should make to God in the traditional sense of finding quiet time to commune, talk, and be with God. The thanksgiving prayer is not a request or desire for anything but one of sincere thanks, gratitude, and appreciation to God for having our issues solved even before we experience them being solved.

What happens when a prayer is not answered?

My belief is that all prayers are answered and come true, because in the space-time continuum, everything seen and unseen that has happened, is currently happening, and can possibly happen in the future, exists. Therefore, whatever I pray about already exists in the space-time continuum. The key is to follow the path from where I am now in the space-time continuum to the place in the space-time continuum where the prayer comes true. People feel that their prayers are not answered because it did not happen in this lifetime. What eventually happens is, during one of their future lifetimes, the prayer will be answered. Therefore, God does answer all prayers, but the answer may not be during our current lifetime.

If God answers all prayers, what happens when I pray for someone not to die and they do?

First of all, I believe no one dies; after they leave their body, they continue to live on but, in essence, that is not the answer to our prayer. If the person dies, it does not mean the prayer was not answered; it only means it does come true during the current lifetime. If, after I die, and I still want that person not to die, I have the option to come back to that place in time in the space-time continuum before their death and take the path along the space-time continuum where the person does not die.

Why aren't prayers answered during our current lifetime?

One reason may be due to the frustration of the road blocks, life issues, and negative thoughts that can take over our mind and cloud our ability to make the right decision for the prayer to be answered, or to readily see the people and things God is sending our way to make it happen.

Another reason may be due to the massive coordination that has to happen involving other people who are needed to answer our prayer. God knows that no one knows everything, so God participates in the co-creation by sending other people into our life. We may be doing all we need to do to have our prayer answered, but if others we need in our life do not get the messages from God, it won't happen in this lifetime.

How can prayers be so all powerful?

If a co-creation prayer (thought, word, action) is in alignment with many other people at the same time, the prayer can come true in a current lifetime. If the same dream by many happens to be one that will change the world to the better, make people's lives better, is a movement toward peace and the greater good, the prayer can be very powerful because it can be answered in a current lifetime or in the next generation.

There have been many examples over my lifetime when the prayer was large and seemingly impossible, but it came true within a generation or has made great strides toward becoming true because many people have the same prayer. Many in the Civil Right Movement had a prayer to improve the lives of African-Americans and minorities, which, in some measure, has come true through many people having the same prayer. The point is that prayers can be very powerful when enough people accept the same prayer.

What is the best way to pray?

There is no right or wrong way to pray a co-creation prayer. Everyone prays every day of their life through their every thought, word, and action. The question is not about the best way to pray but what we are praying about. There is also no best way or time to pray a thanksgiving prayer.

What should we pray about?

We need to be very careful what we pray about because, as the saying goes, be careful what we wish for. Always remember, a co-creation prayer is everything we think, say, and do, which includes all negative thoughts, words, and actions.

I believe prayer is a very powerful tool in the formation of our own lives, the lives of those around us, and how the world is. We need to think, say, and do what we want the world to be like for all future generations of our sisters and brothers. Let's let God know through our thoughts, words, and actions what we really and truly want Heaven on Earth to be like and continue sending out words of gratitude to God for making Earth a place we all can be proud of, by truly accepting and loving our sisters and brothers worldwide as one and treating the Earth and all plants and animals with respect for what they were intended to be here for.

LOVE

What is love?

There is no universal answer to this question. From my research, love is difficult to define because it doesn't denote a single phenomenon, emotion, or feeling. Love is simply too large to grasp through definition, so we all have opinions and thoughts on what is love is, is not, cannot be, and can be.

My definition is that love is a movement toward oneness through positive loving physical action and inaction, positive spoken and unspoken words. The key word in this definition of love is positive. A positive action or positive inaction is a constructive act that draws us nearer to others.

Any action or inaction perceived as negative does not fit into this definition of love due to its destructive nature. A negative action or negative inaction causes a division and rift between us and others.

What are the positive physical actions of love?

Positive physical action can be a gentle hug for no reason; a soft, unexpected kiss; volunteering to lend a helping hand; giving gifts for no reason; a handwritten note of appreciation; or any other physical action that brings positive feelings to the giver and the receiver. A positive physical action has the greatest impact toward oneness when the act is one that is unexpected, unconditional, and not expecting anything in return.

What are the positive physical inactions of love?

This form of love is the type where we give ourselves. A positive physical inaction is controlling our anger in a healthy way and not following through on thoughts of revenge, or refraining from acts of physical harm toward someone who hurts our feelings or causes us emotional pain and trauma. It does not mean we sweep it under the rug, if it is something that needs to be addressed legally. Just don't let negative thoughts prevent us from loving ourselves. It is very difficult to love another unconditionally if we do not love ourselves.

What are the positive spoken words of love?

Loving words and phrases are the most powerful means of creating oneness between two people. The power of oneness can be greatly increased if it is combined with positive physical action. Since we all like to hear those words of "job well done," praise, hope, encouragement, guidance, and support, get in the habit of freely sharing words of kindness with others.

What are the positive unspoken words of love?

There are times when it is best not to say anything, in the name of love. One such situation is when someone close to us has some sort of challenge, issue, or problem. All too often, we sense their anxiety and distress and try to solve their problem because we feel we have to. If they ask for our advice, speak up with loving caution, but providing support by listening with our eyes and being within hand-to-hand contact length is more powerful than offering unsolicited advice. If they feel our support in this way, they will feel more empowered to solve their problem.

Another situation is when someone makes an unintentional mistake and both of us know it. It can be destructive if negative or complaining words are spoken. The best way to handle such situations is to look into their eyes, smile, say nothing, and follow up with loving, positive actions.

If someone is clearly angered to the point of being irrational, it is best not to try and talk to them at that moment. Remain quiet, listen, and give them the space to air out their grievances until they talk themselves out.

As we can see, there are times when supportive words are best kept to ourselves until an appropriate time and place. Choose wisely when and what we say. As powerful and useful as words are, there will be moments when silence is the most powerful way to communicate love.

What does oneness mean as associated with the definition of love?

Oneness is the interconnectedness created between two people, nature, an object, or one's self in a positive physical, emotional, mental, and spiritual way through loving actions or inactions. Anytime there is positive physical action, physical inaction, positive spoken words, or unspoken words between two people, there becomes a connection which can lead to friendship, companionship, or toward the physical, loving interaction of making love, leading to an outpouring of emotional healing, mental happiness, and a spiritual closeness. When this level of oneness (interconnectedness) occurs, it is easy to say "I love you."

Anytime there is positive interaction with nature, a connection can be made in the form of love. Watching a beautiful sunset can become a physical inaction between the viewer and sunset, resulting in closeness through mental peace and, in some cases, spiritual closeness. The simple act of hugging a tree can create oneness and a form of love with a tree. For those who find this hard to comprehend, we may change our mind if we walk up to a giant redwood tree, stretch out our arms against the tree as best we can, and hug the tree. That is why people frequently say "I love this tree," "I love" a sunset, a sunrise, a lightning storm, a moonlit night, etc.

The most important love is the interconnectedness between our conscious mind and our soul. The way to create and intensify this connection is by loving our spouse, friends, co-workers, and strangers, as well as nature and objects. When there is true connection between our soul and conscious mind, we can truly love ourselves and love others unconditionally.

Are we love?

Each of us is who and what we are, as demonstrated by our action, inaction, verbal expression, and non-verbal expression. Love is any positive, loving physical action, physical inaction, positive spoken words, and unspoken words. Therefore, we are love when our actions, inactions, verbal expressions, and non-verbal expressions are positive in nature.

The only time we are not love is if we choose not to love, such as when our physical actions or verbal expressions are negative, which does not cause bonding to another or ourselves.

Is love a choice?

Yes, love is a choice and we all have the freedom to give and receive love. The power to choose, give, and receive love is a precious gift we are born with. Regardless of our social circumstances, race, creed, color, age, handicap, or any other social or physical challenge, we have the ability and right to give and receive love. Love cannot be bought or sold; love is just there for all to give and receive.

When love is chosen, one sees love everywhere and everything we see is looked upon in a positive light. As an example, the sky becomes love by the spoken words or unspoken words in the form of positive thoughts on how pretty the blue sky is or how the clouds look so soft and fluffy. Even if the sky is full of thunderstorms and high winds, the sky is still viewed as love by the positive thoughts of knowing the beauty in the reason for the fierce storm. When choosing love, a table becomes love. From the eyes of love, the form of the table can be seen in a positive light by how functional it is. The texture of the table, the color, and the shape become appealing and seen in a positive light.

On the other hand, if love is not chosen, the sky will not be seen in a positive form or may not even be noticed, thus taken for granted. The fierce storm will be looked upon with negative thoughts on how nasty and destructive it is. The table may also not even be noticed or, if noticed, may be thought of negatively by thinking how the color of the table is ugly or the shape and form is not very pleasing.

When love is chosen, we become one with nature, people, and all things of the world. When love is part of one's life, positive actions are automatic, in helping someone, by being more receptive to receiving physical action, caring more about people, and freely giving hugs of appreciation.

What is the purpose of love?

I believe there is a basic and ultimate purpose of love. The basic purpose is to create earthly oneness with all there is. The ultimate purpose of love is to become one with God, the highest level of love one can experience along the path of love.

What is love to an atheist, agnostic, or some other form of non-theist belief?

God experiences oneness with all human beings on a spiritual level, no matter what our earthly theist or non-theist belief may be. Humans, on the other hand, have a choice to believe in God during this lifetime. Regardless of one's current belief during this lifetime, all humans will eventually achieve earthly oneness with God on a spiritual level.

Those who chose not to believe in a God during this lifetime still have the capacity to love. There are many non-believers who are good people, perform positive physical actions and speak positively and constructively. People who are non-believers still love and create earthly oneness and bonding with themselves and others and have the opportunity to love at three of the four levels of love. The only difference between believers and non-believers is that believers have the opportunity to experience Godly love, whereas non-believers only have the opportunity to experience earthly love.

What must be in place for love to occur?

With love, there must be a willing giver and an accepting receiver. There has to be someone who initiates the love and one who willingly or unwillingly receives the love. The receiver doesn't have to reciprocate for it to be love, but the receiver has the choice to give love back to the giver. If all our decisions are made from love, there would be unity and oneness with all humankind and thus, ultimately, with God.

How can one experience love?

Love is a choice. It takes two for love to exist. There is a path of love that we travel during our lifetime. Along this path of love are four levels of love. Each level builds toward oneness with humankind and, thus, with God. Each level also helps one become better equipped emotionally and mentally to choose and become love. If one does not choose love, then the probability of achieving oneness is not very high, defeating what I see as the purpose of love and our purpose for being in physical form on Earth.

Does love grow?

Yes, love does grow. From the moment of conception to the moment of death, there is a path of love traveled by all. That path has four natural levels of love we can experience, in various depths and degrees, during our lifetime. It is important we experience each level to the fullest extent possible before moving to the next level.

Each level is a building block to the next. The more love is developed at each level, the more solid the foundation we have in working our way through the next level. It is not impossible to go from one level to the next without growth, but growth makes the next level easier. Humans have a finite capacity to achieve total growth at all levels of love; love is too big, and earthly life in one lifetime is too short.

It is these deficiencies at each level that cause problems in the higher levels of love. Though we may experience problems in higher levels of love, it does not mean we cannot go back and fix the problems from earlier levels of love.

There is no defining line that signals we have learned all we can and it's time to move to the next level. The movement along the path of love is a natural evolution from one level to the next.

Though the order listed is sequential, one may experience more than one level at a time, with the exception of developmental love and Godly love, which require all previous levels of love to be experienced first.

The hierarchy of love on the path of love are: developmental, self, human, and Godly.

What is developmental love?

A child receives developmental life from their caregivers during the time between infancy to adolescence. Caregivers of developmental love include parents, guardians, family members, friends, nannies, day care centers, child care takers, school counselors, therapist, and others. Children continue to receive developmental love beyond adolescence, but its effectiveness dwindles as the youth ages. Receiving developmental love is very important because the quantity and, more importantly, the quality of developmental love a child receives affects all other levels of love, emotional growth, and mental health throughout the child's life. The goal of developmental love is for the child to receive love and thus know they are loved.

Children first receive developmental love after birth, in the form of the warmth and security of the mother's arms and from being fed. As the child develops from infancy to adolescence, they receive other types of unconditional developmental love in the form of hugs, kisses, protection from harm, being listened to, being allowed a voice, and other actions and words. The love a child's mind feels by receiving developmental love is total bliss and is a big step toward the child being emotionally stable and mentally healthy.

On the other hand, one can very easily see how a child who did not receive an acceptable level of developmental love can develop emotional problems and adverse personality traits. Therefore, one can see how the receiving of developmental love at this stage of life is a form of love that is very important and beneficial at this stage of a child's life.

The biological parents or guardians of children are the most influential givers of developmental love. But regardless who provides the developmental love, the important issue is that they know they are loved.

What is love during the developmental love stage?

Love is any positive:

- physical action, including hugs, kisses, bathing, clothing, protecting, and providing.

- physical inaction, including refraining from causing physical harm.

- spoken words, including saying "I love you" and praising the child

- unspoken words, as in refraining from saying discouraging words or speaking out

What is self-love?

Self-love is taking care of ourselves mentally, physically, intellectually, spiritually, and socially. Self-love is very important because, as mentioned before, we can fully love another if we don't love ourselves, but to be able to love someone unconditionally, we need to love ourselves.

What is human love?

Human love is the level of love most humans relate to. This is the type of love that is non-platonic and involves romance, dating, relationships, marriage, sex, intimacy, passion, and the mysterious attraction of falling in love. We generally experience human love as teenagers and it continues throughout our life. Similar to self-love, there is not a clear point when one begins to experience human love.

At the beginning of this level, the degree of developmental love from a caregiver still exists but the impact drops off dramatically. Though the caregivers' interaction has less and less of an impact, the ability to experience human love is greatly dependent upon the foundation of developmental love. Human love can be very confusing, difficult to experience, and, at this level, there is an overlapping of self-love and human love.

Human love falls in the natural hierarchy of love after self-love, but when human love is experienced to a greater degree than self-love, unhealthy conflict can occur—one must have self-love before they can unconditionally give it to another.

What is Godly love?

Godly love is the highest level of love. Godly love contains all three other levels of love. With Godly love, there is the total ultimate feeling of oneness with all. Even though we all have the potential to achieve this level of love, I believe only a very few have experienced Godly love, such as Muhammad, Jesus, Buda, Gandhi, Krishna, the Dalai Lama, and Mother Theresa.

In my belief, Godly love is the level of love toward which all the human souls strive. The soul's overall grand plan is for all of humankind to be one with each other and, thus, one with God. But before we can achieve Godly love, we strive to follow our individual mission while in the physical body on Earth. The purpose of an individual's mission in life is to live their life in alignment with the soul's mission while being part of the physical body on Earth.

What is unconditional love?

Traditionally, unconditional love is loving others with the expectation of receiving nothing in return, with no boundaries or limits. One expresses unconditional love to another not because they have to, but because they want to. My problem with this definition is that it seems to fulfill a desire to love another unconditionally in order to satisfy our senses. To me, what occurs when loving unconditionally under these pretenses is that, over time, there will become a point when there will not be the same level of fulfillment of the senses, which can result in an individual slipping away from loving unconditionally.

Another definition of unconditional love is not defining it as an action but as an individual state of being and thinking. Under this definition, unconditional love is not possible without first unconditionally loving oneself. There are those who have written that it is possible to love another without loving oneself and, to an extent, I agree, but to unconditionally love another, we must first unconditionally love ourselves.

So, to me, loving another unconditionally is a spiritual love, which, as a state of being, is the highest and most powerful form of love. By loving from a state of being in this spiritual way, I accept that we are all one, worldwide, regardless of race, creed, color, or culture and we are all on this incredible journey together.

How can parents of murderers love their children unconditionally?

A mother and father can love their children unconditionally based on who they were, not what they turned into. Hideous killers, like Charles Manson and Hitler, were not born killers but were young and innocent children loved by their parents unconditionally, whether, because of social cultural condition, belief system cultural conditioning, a mental illness or some other factors, their children became someone else.

How does one begin loving themselves unconditionally from a spiritual state of being?

The profound unconditional love of self begins when we first unconditionally forgive and accept ourselves from our limiting beliefs systems, destructive social and cultural conditioning, stupid mistakes, judgments of self, and misunderstandings. I had to joyfully correct my errors, set myself free, clear my conscience, take a deep breath, and start a new life of profound unconditional love of self by forgiving and accepting myself for who I really am.

Then I needed return to who I am, what I am here for, my purpose in life, my talents, and be who and what I am here on Earth for, rather than listening to and following what others think I should or should not be.

THE FUTURE

Will humans eventually eliminate themselves from the face of the Earth?

Prior to the nuclear age, humans did not possess the capability of a self-imposed global extinction. Unfortunately, humankind is now at a very crucial point in its existence because we not only have the nuclear capability, but also biological capabilities to eliminate all life forms. I do not believe humans will eliminate themselves from the face of the Earth, but there is still the strong possibility that there may be a nuclear or biological event. Even though the thought of a nuclear and biological attack sounds extremely frightening, I see no reason to live in fear, because our spirit never dies and lives on forever.

Why won't humans not eliminate themselves from the planet?

I feel humans will not eliminate themselves from the planet because, statistically, the world is becoming less and less violent. Harvard psychologist, Steven Pinker, says in his book <u>The Better Angels of Our Nature: Why Violence Has Declined</u> that, historically, we've never had it this peaceful. His statistics indicate there has been a very dramatic reduction in war deaths, family violence, racism, rape, murder, and all sorts of mayhem.

I also believe the world is coming to the realization of how destructive the next big war will be. A deterrent to war is to create a situation where the negative consequences outweigh the positive or gain to be made. Humankind and leaders of the countries with the nuclear and biological weapons understand this and will not push the button to start the end of human life on Earth.

Do humans have the capability of destroying the Earth?

I think humans have the capability of eliminating humans and all other animal and plant life forms from the Earth, but humans will never be able to destroy Earth. Mother Earth is extremely powerful, resourceful, and has mind-boggling resurrection and recovery capabilities. In the past 4.5 billion years, the Earth has recovered from ice ages, natural disasters, asteroids, comets, bursts of gamma-rays from distance galaxies, and other calamities. Humans do have the ability to destroy themselves from the Earth by whatever means, but if humans are eliminated, the Earth will adapt, resurrect, recover, and continue to evolve and exist forever, regardless if humans are around or not.

What is going to happen in the next 100 years?

The next 100 years will be the most challenging, exciting, and impactful years in the history of human existence on Earth because of technological advancements, such as the use of artificial intelligence in creating intelligent machines.

I do not believe there will be a nuclear or biological war in the next 100 years. I do believe there is the very high probability of an isolated nuclear or biological attack from an extremist group, but it will not eliminate humankind. The attack will be of such a magnitude that it will cause a great setback for humankind worldwide, but it will provide a cold enough slap in the face that it will not happen again.

What are artificial intelligence (AI) and super artificial intelligence machines?

AI machines are already a mainstay and are making a very positive impact on all of humankind. AI includes search engines, GPS, cell phones, autopilots, computers, and many other devices. I believe we will have super-intelligent robot-type machines that exceed human-level skills. It will lead to human-like machines that can learn, think, and solve problems on their own and be smarter than those considered as geniuses in their field of expertise. Upon reaching human-level intelligence, there will be a continuous creative feedback loop between super-intelligent machines that will boost their intelligence further and further beyond human capabilities.

How will AI and super-intelligent machines make a positive impact within the next 100 years?

AI and super-intelligent machines will produce mindboggling and positive outcomes for humanity worldwide and in preservation of the Earth including:

- The end of hunger, by creating as well as growing healthy and nutritious food at a very low cost.

- Clean energy that will eliminate air and water pollution. Advances in harvesting the sun's rays into much more powerful and inexpensive solar power will eliminate all existing energy sources currently used.

- Elimination of diseases through quick diagnosis and development of cures.

- Safer travel due to driverless vehicles and fully-automated planes as well as flight control.

- More accurate predictions of natural disasters, including tornados, earthquakes, and tsunamis to prevent mass loss of life

- More access to knowledge and information leading to humanity worldwide becoming smarter.

How will humans become smarter and smarter?

Humans will have access to all the information they currently have access to without the use of a computer. Improving intelligence and become smarter is typically achieved by access to information and data. Now, we have access to almost any kind of information we desire via our phones, tablets, and personal computers. I envision that in the future, our brains will be able to access the cloud in the same fashion as our computers are doing today and get whatever information we need by just thinking about it.

If humans become smarter, won't we be on the same level as AI machines?

No. The greatest advantage AI and super-intelligent machines have over the human brain at its current size, is unlimited capacity to gather, process, and store enormous amount of data and information.

What about humans' negative environmental impact?

We negatively impact the environment because our rate of intellectual, mental, and sociological evolution and spiritual growth isn't advanced enough to solve these problems. The good news is we have help on the way in the form of advanced information technology (IT) and artificial intelligence to help speed our ability to solve these problems.

We will be able to rapidly find technological ways to prevent humankind from negatively impacting the ozone layer, air, and water. Advanced IT and artificial intelligence will also help eliminate the need for deforestation, help with population control, help in creating healthy food forms, clean energy, and the list goes on and on.

How can IT and AI be our way out of the existing and future problems?

We have always heard the saying that knowledge is all powerful. This is very true, but the collective brain power of all humanity is not powerful enough to wrap our minds around solving these problems in an expedient manner. This is where advance computers married with artificial intelligence come into the picture, to process the information at incredible speeds to create solutions to our self-made human problems within the next several decades.

Consider that in the 1970s, a state-of-the-art computer took up a room. The technology and computer power in a smart phone is 1,000 times more powerful. The growth of informational technology and artificial intelligence will continue to grow exponentially and I think, in 25 years, they will be a billion times more powerful than today.

Won't it be exciting when the infinite processing and operational capabilities of super-intelligent machines are used in concert with genuine human love and compassion to eliminate starvation, extreme poverty, and human neglect worldwide, no matter our race, creed, or belief system?

Is it possible that artificial intelligence will create problems for humankind?

Intellectual machines will not cause lasting problems or be an imminent lasting threat. I foresee a day in the distant future when robots are more intelligent than humans. There will become a time when it will be hard to distinguish between intelligent machines and humans. These intelligent machines will become a new species on Earth. Unlike humans, these intellectual machines will not create their own problems from ideas and inventions that are intended to serve humanity in a positive way.

Even if humans' program into an intelligent machine or if an intelligent machine does go rogue, there will be a built-in algorithm to prevent any rogue intelligent machine from creating havoc.

Humans have always reached out to grow as a species mentally, intellectually, physically, and socially, as well as from a technological and industrial viewpoint. This began with the cavemen. It continues to progress and advance today and will continue. Each time there is a reaching out, there will be advantages and disadvantages that followed. But history has shown that each advancement has proven to be more of an advantage than disadvantage.

There will be challenges and concerns with creating a species of intelligent machines, but in the end, these machines to will have a far greater impact for good on the human way of life than we can imagine today.

What will prevent intelligent machines from taking over the planet?

Prior to these intelligent machines reaching the point of thinking and putting in place the process of thought, word, and action and creating on their own, people and countries involved in the development of superintelligence will create a way to prevent machines from rebelling against humans. They will be programmed to know we are all one in terms of working together for the better good of each other, value human life, understand it was humans who created them, Earth is their home, and that humans are only transient visitors to Earth, as they will be moving to another place in the space-time continuum after dying.

Won't AI superintelligence result in job loss?

There are jobs already being lost due to artificial super-intelligent machines and robots but other jobs are being created. These jobs include maintaining the robots, construction of the robots, creating the products built into the robots, etc. History has shown technological advancements in the past not only caused loss of jobs but also created new industries and jobs.

With the rapid growth of artificial superintelligence reaching an exponential pace, there will be a period of time in the near future where new jobs for humans will not be created and fewer and fewer jobs will be available for humans. In the end, robots will be doing all the work and there will be no need for money. Humans will be able to go about creating a life to serve their purpose on Earth.

There will be a period of time during the transition of labor to artificial super intelligent machines and robots were money is still needed but there will be no jobs available. To help during this transition, there will be a fund set up by the new World Government that will be available for those needing money and no jobs being created. The primary source of these funds will be from the military budgets currently in place by all the countries around the world. During this transition, war but eventually become nonexistent because the reasons for war will no longer exist. Currently, the United States has budgeted $598 billion for defense spending with the next 14 countries totaling $666 billion and the remaining countries $317 billion. This totals to $1.579 trillion available, more than enough to source out.

Why won't there be any wars in the distant future?

There will not be a need for any county to go to war because the reasons for war will no longer exist. One reason a country or group goes to war is for more land to expand their empire. In the future, there will be no need to expand their empire because the world will have one world government. Currently, each country has their own governing body but, in the future, I envision there will be a United World government, which will preside over all of the current countries but allow each individual country keep their cultures and way of life, just like the US federal government oversees fifty individual states.

Wars also start in order to control mineral and energy resources. In the future, there will not be a need for oil or gas due to the unlimited source of power from the sun. Solar energy advancement will be at a level that will provide all the energy needed to provide electricity to home, offices, and all other buildings. Automobiles and all other forms of transportation, including airplanes, will all be solar powered.

War also happens because one country feels superior to another or hates their way of life. In the future, there will different countries but all under the United World government; thus, there will not be any countries to overrun since all countries will be as one.

Another reason for wars is to eliminate a group or sect of people due to differences in religious faith, killing in the name of their God. In the future, there will not necessarily be one world religion, but a level of core beliefs that all religions share while keeping their current belief system and way of worship intact. There will still be atheists and agnostics, which will be accepted by all other religions, while the core belief taught by all religions will be as follows:

- There is a God consisting of unlimited love.

- God is not to be feared.

- There is no such place as a physical Hell.

- We are all are spirits and when we die, our spirit lives on.

- No one religion or belief system is superior to another.

- Killing, harming, or verbally abusing and condemning anyone, no matter their race, culture, or religious belief, is unacceptable.

- No culture, race, or person is superior to or inferior to another.

- Teach about social/cultural conditioning.

- Teach about living a life and being a person of high integrity.

- Share and announce all the good news there is.

Where does God and the human soul/spirit fit in the future?

Nothing will change, regardless of advanced AI. We will always be creative; we are one continuous creative spirit. Prior to being incarnated in the body as a soul, we create our purpose. While a soul, we continue the creative process through thought, word, and action. And even when we die, we create our own Heaven and our own afterlife.

Spirits will continue to be incarnated into a human body upon conception as a soul. The soul/spirit will still have a purpose on Earth as well as being a messenger, provider of a service, and/or teacher to others. Humans will continue to have the free will of choice and continue being the creative being they are through thought, word, and action. The spirit will still continue experiencing the decisions made by the body-mind-soul triune in order to experience all there is to know, so that the pieces of God, which is the daughter and son spirits of God, and God can know and understand all that It knows conceptually.

Will there become a time when technology prevents humans from dying?

Yes, there will come a time when humans will no longer die of old age, diseases, or illnesses and the mind, body, and soul/spirit will have the ability live on Earth forever. Then, it will be the spirit of the human triune of body, mind, and soul/spirit that will decide when it is time for the mind and body to die and the spirit to be born again into the afterlife. The moment in time the spirit makes this decision will be when the soul/spirit has served its purpose for coming to Earth in the first place.

Will there ever be peace on Earth?

Absolutely, there will eventually be peace on Earth. The time will be in the distant future when there is a complete and peaceful merger of the super intelligence of artificial machines with the genuine feeling, emotions, and love of the human soul/spirit. Spirits in the distant future will have experienced all there is to experience and conceptually understand all there is, but spirits will still elect to be incarnated again as souls on Earth to totally enjoy all the beauty and splendor Earth has available to everyone. Earth will become a vacation place for all the spirits.

As mentioned before, to move humankind along toward a life of peace on Earth is to address the areas of influence by upgrading our organized religions, addressing the social and cultural conditioning issues, and each individual moving toward living a life of high integrity.

Therefore, the answer the question on what is holding humankind back from living a life of peace on Earth now without artificial intelligence is all of us.

CONCLUSION

Thank you for taking the time to read *Questions About... The Great Mysteries of Life and Beyond Life.* I really loved every minute of what seemed to be never-ending journey because one question led to another and another and another. I didn't mind, because I had no timeline, and the purpose of this book was only the pure joy and thrill of exploring and finding my belief system and a level of peace with all there is.

My wish for you is to find your own belief system, whatever it may be. I would be honored if you came up with your own answers to the question presented in this book and especially honored if you came up with answers to other questions not mentioned in this book.

www.ingramcontent.com/pod-product-compliance
Lightning Source LLC
LaVergne TN
LVHW020930090426
835512LV00020B/3299